This is Hinduism

Dave Symmons

First published in 1998 by:
Stanley Thornes (Publishers) Ltd
Delta Place
27 Bath Road
Cheltenham GL53 7TH
United Kingdom

06 / 10 9 8

A catalogue record for this book is available from the British
Library.

ISBN 0-7487-3093-1

Printed and bound in China by Midas Printing International Ltd.

Acknowledgements

With thanks to the following for permission to reproduce
photographs and illustrations:

Andes Press Agency/Carlos Reyez-Manzo 26, 34, 35, 42 (top),
67 ● Simon Conti 8 (bottom) ● Sally Greenhill 57 ● The
Hutchison Library 14 (top), 22, 24, 50, 56, 95; /Tim Beddow 28;
/Bernard Gérard 65; /John Hatt 29; /Liba Taylor 30, 36, 40, 41,
51, 88 ● Christine Osborne Pictures 9, 17, 19, 27; /C Milne 8
(top) ● Ann & Bury Peerless 6, 12, 14 (bottom), 15, 16, 18, 20,
21, 32, 42 (bottom), 52, 64, 68, 81, 82, 90, 91, 92, 93 ● Rex
Features 72 ● Sathya Sai Book Centre of UK, London 60 ●
Dave Symmons 87 ● Jerry Wooldridge 33.

Every effort has been made to contact copyright holders and
we apologise if any have been inadvertently overlooked.

Design and page make-up by Janet McCallum.

Illustrated by Gillian Hunt and Mike Land.

Cover artwork by Ian Kennedy.

Picture research by Simon Conti.

Throughout this book the terms BCE (Before Common Era)
and CE (Common Era) are used instead of the more familiar
BC and AD. However, in practice, they mean the same thing.

Contents

1 Introduction
What is Hinduism?

Hinduism could be described as one of the world's oldest religions, dating back some 3,000 years or more. The name 'Hindu' was given to describe the people who lived near the River Indus in India: the word 'Indus' became 'Hindu'. These people did not all believe the same things, but there were enough similarities to start talking about Hindus. However, many Hindus would prefer to call their religion '**Sanatan Dharma**'. Hinduism is not defined by beliefs: you are born Hindu and cannot really become one.

Beliefs

Hindus believe in one God, but Hinduism has two to three hundred million **deities**, each representing a different aspect of God. Hindus believe in **reincarnation** and in **moksha**. In this book we shall look at some of the things that a great many Hindus have in common.

Spellings

The way some Hindu words are spelled may vary. The words have been phonetically translated into English: this means that if you say the word out loud it will sound the same, whichever spelling you see. For example, **Divali** is sometimes spelled Diwali, Diwalee or Deepawali. You might therefore see different spellings in other books, shop windows, cards, etc.

- What does the word 'deity' mean?
- Why are some Hindu words spelled differently?
- What name do Hindus give to their faith?

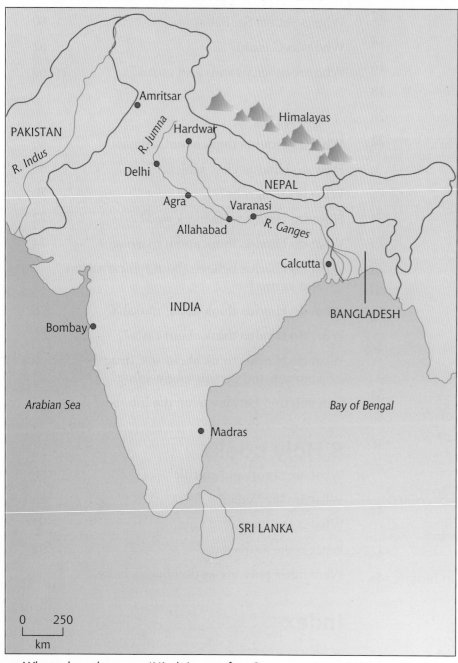

Where does the name 'Hindu' come from?

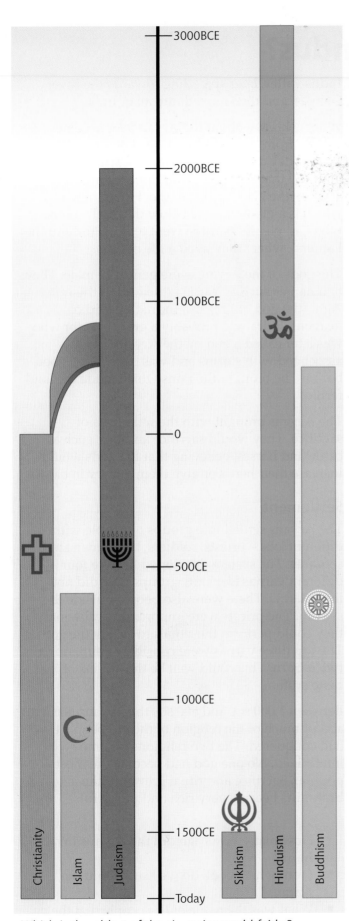

Which is the oldest of the six major world faiths?

For your dictionary

Deity is another word for God or gods.

Divali is the festival of lights and marks the beginning of the New Year in the Hindu calendar.

Moksha means 'release' and refers to the release from having to be reborn.

Om or **aum** is the most sacred Hindu syllable and sound.

Reincarnation is the belief that when you die you can be reborn again on earth.

Sanatan Dharma means the eternal religion of Hinduism. Hindus often prefer this term as it shows that the religion has always existed and always will.

1 In your own words, explain why the word 'Hindu' is both right and wrong when describing this religion.

2 Why do you think that some Hindus prefer the term 'Sanatan Dharma'?

3 This symbol is pronounced **om** or **aum** – a sacred sound in Hinduism. Hindus believe it is the sound of God, and most accept it as the symbol of their religion.

a   Copy the symbol carefully into your book.
b   Label it 'Om' or 'Aum'.
c   If it does not offend you, say the word out loud.

5

Who were the first Hindus?

About 3,500 years ago, the people who lived around the River Indus were known as **Dravidians**. They were invaded from the north by a group of people we call **Aryans**. It is this mixture of Dravidian and Aryan beliefs which has created Hinduism.

The Dravidians

Before the Aryan invasion there were people living near the River Indus. They built one or two large cities but most of the people lived in villages. People had their own God (whom some people now claim was **Shiva**) and goddesses (which were worshipped to make the crops grow). The Dravidians worshipped fertility symbols and animals such as the bull. They believed in **karma** and that who you were was affected by what you had done in a previous life.

The Aryan invasion

The Aryans came from what is now called central Asia and the south of Russia. They came first to the Indus valley, later spreading towards the River Ganges, and then moved into all of India.

What is known about the Aryan people comes mainly from the sacred writings known as **Rig Veda**. They did not believe in reincarnation. They believed that those who had done wrong were sent, by the god Varuna, to the 'House of Clay', which is a gloomy place below the earth. Those who had pleased Varuna went to the 'World of the Fathers', where they lived a life of bliss.

The gods of the Aryans were generally male. They had names such as Varuna (the lord of the waters), Agni (the god of fire) and Indra (the lord of heaven). Indra was probably a great warrior who was later called a god by the Aryans. He was associated with storms and was considered good because he brought the rains which made the land fertile.

The Aryans brought with them the idea of sacrifice. They would sacrifice animals, such as cattle and horses, believing that the gods would increase their herds or give them victory in battle.

Settlement

The Aryans settled into groups of people with different jobs – priests, soldiers, tradesmen and servants. The system developed to have four different **varnas** (separate groups who did not intermarry). There were also people outside the system. The priests were important because only they could perform the rituals to satisfy the gods. The top three varnas were considered superior, or **twice-born**. This could well be the origins of the **caste** system.

Between 1,000 BCE and 500 BCE the Aryans began to accept much of the religion of the the people they had conquered. The two religions became intermixed. No one god had become the most popular. Sacrifice and ritual grew and the **brahmins** became very rich and powerful.

- How many years ago did the Aryans invade India?
- From which book do we learn about the Aryans?
- What was the name of the people that the Aryans conquered?

People today still worship Shiva as a symbol of fertility. What do you think is happening in this picture?

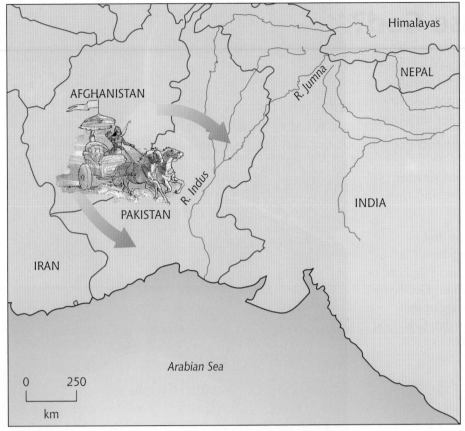

Where did the Aryans came from and where did they go?

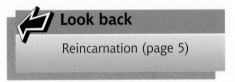

Look back

Reincarnation (page 5)

For your dictionary

The **Aryans** ('noble people') were the people who invaded India in about 1,500 BCE.

A **brahmin** is a Hindu priest, responsible for the performance of rituals and teaching the scriptures.

The **caste** system is the division of Hindu society into separate classes of people.

The **Dravidians** were a race of people who lived near the River Indus.

Karma means 'actions' or 'deeds'. It refers to the belief that what a person does in this life leads to rewards or punishments in the next life.

Rig Veda is the first and most sacred of all the Hindu scriptures.

Shiva is one of the greatest of the Hindu gods.

Some religious people believe that you work up through the caste system depending on your karma. The top three castes are often called the **twice-born** as they have already lived a life as a shudra (unskilled worker).

A **varna** is one of the four main groups in Hindu society. Castes are subdivisions within each varna.

1 a Draw a timeline to show the Aryan invasion. Include at least three events for each date on the timeline.

b Draw a picture to illustrate each event.

2 Complete the following sentences by matching the beginnings on the left with the correct ending on the right.

The Dravidians — was a gloomy place below the earth.

The Aryans conquered — horses to their gods.

The Aryans sacrificed — the land around the River Indus.

The 'House of Clay' — were farming people who lived near the River Indus.

Gods

How do we sense God?

All religions find it difficult to describe God. This is not surprising, because if we could describe God perfectly, God would probably not be very impressive. Hindus often talk about sensing God or using your senses to find God.

If you have difficulty in thinking about sensing God, try to understand the thinking behind this Hindu:

'Do you believe that God can be anywhere and in anything? If God cannot be in everything then God would be limited and so would not be God. If God can be in anything, pick up a stone and think about God being in that stone. If you can imagine God being in that stone, then you can use that stone to worship God. God is not the stone but the stone can be a help in understanding God. God can be in that stone!'

The five senses

Sound

The sound of God is described as om or aum. The sound is a bit like that of breathing, or the noise made by blowing into a conch shell.

Sight

Hindus often use objects to help them 'see' God. Many of the statues that they use in their **mandirs** are thought to represent God. Some have many arms and others have animal heads or bodies. In some services they use a coconut to represent God. The objects are there to help them to visualise God.

Smell

In homes and in mandirs, Hindus may burn **ghee** lamps and incense. These smells do not represent the smell of God but they sweeten the air and help people to focus on God.

A golden conch shell outside a temple in India. Why are conch shells special?

How do you picture God?

In what way is food an important symbol in Hinduism?

For your dictionary

Arti is a part of Hindu worship where a tray of lamps is passed amongst worshippers.
Ghee is clarified butter. It is used in cooking and to fuel lamps.
A **mandir** is a Hindu temple.
Prashad is food offered to the gods and then distributed amongst worshippers.

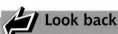 **Look back**

Om (page 5)

- What is om?
- What is burnt to make the mandirs smell sweet?
- What is prashad?

Taste

Many Hindus will tell you about the importance of taste. Food has to be prepared carefully, with a sense of peace, and offered to God before it is eaten. Visitors to a mandir are given **prashad**. Worship may involve drinking a little liquid which has been offered to the gods.

Touch

Touch is a very important sense. As babies, we all touch and feel things to help us to make sense of them. In **arti** ceremonies, worshippers often move their hands through the holy flames and then touch their foreheads. In this way they are bringing the holy light into their lives.

1 If you were to eat something to remind you of God, what would that be? Why have you chosen this particular food?

2 If God could be understood by touch, what would God be like? Explain your answer.

3 Find an object which makes you feel peaceful when you touch it and explain why.

4 If it does not offend you, draw a picture of an object which could represent God. Explain why you have drawn this object.

5 What smell makes you think of holy things? If God had to be represented as a smell, what would it be? Explain your answer.

How many gods?

There is one God in Hinduism – **Brahman**, the Supreme Spirit. Brahman is not male or female, animal or human, but the spirit from which everything comes and into which everything will disappear. The many other gods and goddesses worshipped in Hinduism each make up a different part of Brahman.

Understanding God

We can try to understand God if we think about light passing through a prism and coming out the other side. Light entering the prism (Brahman) splits into the colours of the rainbow when it leaves the prism (the many gods and goddesses). Of course, there are only seven colours in the rainbow, but there are said to be more than 200 million gods in Hinduism. Each of these gods is still part of the One God, Brahman.

Brahma, Shiva and Vishnu

There are three main, powerful deities worshipped by Hindus:

- **Brahma** is the four-faced creator God.

- **Vishnu** is the preserver God. He has four arms and holds a conch shell. From age to age he visits the earth to remove evil and to let good flourish.

- Shiva may seem to many people to be dangerous and frightening because he is the destroyer God. However, destruction is necessary to allow new things to happen. Shiva is not to be feared because he destroys but should be worshipped for allowing new things to happen.

For your dictionary
Brahma is the creator God.
Brahman is the Supreme Spirit, which is shown through all the other gods and goddesses.
Vishnu is the preserver God.

- Who is the Supreme Spirit?
- Why do many gods and goddesses exist?
- Which three gods create, preserve and destroy all life?

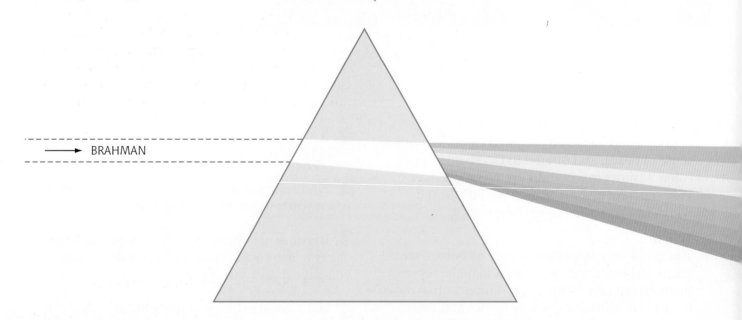

BRAHMAN

How can light passing through a prism explain the idea of God?

Brahma

Vishnu

Shiva

How do these three gods keep the universe in balance?

Look back

Deity (page 5)
Shiva (page 7)

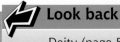

Brahma

Vishnu

Shiva

Ganesha

Hanuman

Rama

Krishna

1 This story is often told to explain the idea of the Supreme Spirit and the many gods:

Six blind wise men [sages] discover an elephant for the very first time in their lives. Each of the sages touches a different part of the elephant and then calls out to tell the others what an elephant is like. The one touching the tail says, 'I am certain that an elephant is like a piece of rope.' The sage touching the leg says, 'I am certain that an elephant is like a tree trunk.' The third sage touches the side of the elephant and says, 'You are both mistaken; the elephant is like a huge wall.' The fourth touching the ear says, 'How can you be so wrong? An elephant is like the sail on a boat.' The fifth sage touches the elephant's trunk and laughs at the others, saying, 'You are trying to trick me; an elephant is like a huge snake.' The last blind sage touches the tusk and says, 'An elephant is like a smooth rock.'

a Which sage was correct?
b How does this story help to explain how Hindus can have the One God but many gods?

2 Why do you think that Hindus cannot make a picture of the Supreme Spirit but they can make pictures and drawings of the many gods?

3 Draw three pictures to represent destruction, creation and preservation. Underneath each picture write a sentence or two to explain what you think needs to be destroyed, preserved and created in this world.

Who is Vishnu?

Vishnu is known as the preserver God. He helps to keep the earth from being destroyed or taken over by evil. Hindus have stories which tell of Vishnu visiting this planet nine times and they expect him to visit one more time in the future. They call the person – or animal – in which he visits this planet an **avatar**. Therefore, we can say that Vishnu has visited this planet as nine different avatars.

Who is Vishnu?

The story of Narasimha

The world was taken over by an evil demon called Hiranyakashyapu. He had tricked the creator God, Brahma, into making him virtually immortal. No man or animal could kill him: he could not die during the day or in the night, he could not be killed on the earth or in the sky and he could not be killed by fire, water, or any weapon. He thought that he was safe from death.

Narasimha (the fourth avatar of Vishnu) came to the earth. He was half-human and half-lion (but neither human nor animal). He caught the demon in the evening (neither day nor night), he lifted him across his thigh (neither on the earth nor in the sky) and he tore him to pieces with his claws (not fire, water or weapon). So the world was once again saved from an evil demon.

> **⬅ Look back**
>
> Brahma (page 10)
> Vishnu (page 10)

The avatars of Vishnu

1 Matsya – a giant fish who saved the world from a flood

2 Kurma – a tortoise who carried the whole world on his back

3 Varaha – a boar who lifted the world out of deep waters using his tusks

4 Narasimha – a half-man and half-lion who killed a demon

5 Vamana – a dwarf who saved the world from an evil demon king

6 Parashurama – known as Rama with an axe

7 **Rama** – a prince who had many adventures, which appear in an epic story called the **Ramayana**

8 **Krishna** – a prince who had many adventures from the moment of his birth

9 **Buddha** – a prince who gave up his wealth and started Buddhism

10 Kalki – will come as a warrior on a white horse to end the present 'age of darkness'

- Why is Vishnu called the preserver god?
- How many times has he visited this earth?
- Which avatar has yet to come to earth?

1 This is what three Hindus think about stories like the one about Narasimha:

'All these stories tell us something about God. Many of them have a historical basis – a prince called Rama certainly existed. They are like legends, based on true stories but changed to make the point.'

'Yes, the stories are all true. Some people do not believe them these days because we are in the "age of darkness".'

'In the old days people used to tell stories and many of them have been written down. It does not matter if they are true or not because they show us how God looks after us.'

These three views can be called literal, mythical and parable. Copy the statements above and write either literal, mythical or parable alongside them. (You might need a dictionary to help you.)

2 *'Whenever there is decay of righteousness... then I Vishnu will come forth... for the protection of the good and the destruction of evil doers.'*

(Bhagavad Gita 4:7,8)

Copy this extract into your book and explain in your own words what it means.

3 a What do you notice about the sequence of the avatars? (Clue: What are the first and last?)
b What does this tell us about them?

Who is Shiva?

The word 'shiv' means 'good', so Shiva is 'the good'. Shiva is shown in many different ways, but there are three main forms that Hindu pictures and statues take: seated with a trident, Shiva linga and Shiva nataraj.

Symbols

There are many important symbols in these pictures:

- The cobra. This shows that Shiva is beyond the power of death and that he is not afraid to die. In fact, the cobra protects him.

- The trident. This is a powerful weapon of death. The three prongs show how the three gods, Brahma, Vishnu and Shiva, work together to create, preserve and destroy life.

- The tiger skin. Again, this shows how Shiva is beyond the power of death. Once in the forest he was attacked by a tiger, but he killed it with his bare hands and used the skin as a coat.

- The matted hair. Shiva is Lord of the Wind and his matted hair is a symbol of the wind. In another story, Shiva let the River Ganges flow through his hair to allow it to pour out of heaven and onto the earth.

Shiva with a trident (a three-pronged weapon)

- Three horizontal lines. This can have many meanings but it is usually to remind Hindus of the three gods Shiva, Brahma and Vishnu.

A story about Shiva

Shiva was sitting in Kailasa, a heavenly place in the Himalayas, teaching his wife, **Parvati**, about the **Vedas**. After a long time, she lost concentration. This annoyed Shiva and he threw her out of Kailasa and sent her to live on earth as a fisherwoman. Shiva was immediately sorry for what he had done, but, as she was now of a different caste to him, he could not just go and get her. She would have to be given to him by her earthly father. Shiva was lonely for many years.

Shiva's servant was called Nandi. Nandi saw that his master was unhappy and so he worked out a plan to get the two back together. He changed into a big fish and swam around the waters where Parvati

Shiva linga (the word 'ling' means 'giver of life')

Shiva nataraj (performing a cosmic dance to control the universe)

For your dictionary

Parvati is the wife of Shiva and is worshipped in many different forms.

The **Vedas** are a collection of four of the oldest Hindu holy books.

- What does the word 'Shiva' mean?
- Who was Parvati?
- Who was Nandi?

Look back

Brahma (page 10)
Caste (page 7)
Reincarnation (page 5)
Shiva (page 7)
Vishnu (page 10)

was now living. Nandi tipped over the fishing boats and scared all the fishermen and women.

The chief of the fisherpeople organised a competition. The man who could kill the big fish would be able to marry his daughter, Parvati. Parvati prayed to Shiva so that the right man for her would win. Shiva heard the prayers and came down to earth so that he could enter the competition. On the day of the contest, many young men tried and failed to kill the big fish. Shiva was the last to try and he destroyed the big fish. Shiva married Parvati and carried her back to Kailasa.

But what became of Nandi, the servant who had become the big fish? This story illustrates the idea of destroying to create. The fish was destroyed to create happiness for Shiva and Parvati. Nandi was reincarnated to become the servant of Shiva again.

1 Look at the three pictures of Shiva. Say in your own words what each picture represents.

2 Copy one of the pictures of Shiva and label it.

3 In this crossword you have the answers but the clues are missing. Make up your own short clues to go with each answer.

15

Who is Krishna?

Krishna is the eighth avatar of Vishnu (see pages 12 and 13). There are many stories about Krishna. Some of them are in the **Bhagavad Gita** (see pages 90 and 91). Many Hindus are very devoted to Krishna. You will read about a group called the International Society for Krishna Consciousness on pages 64 and 65.

Look back

Avatar (page 13)
Krishna (page 13)
Vishnu (page 10)

How did Krishna kill Putna?

Early years

Krishna's parents were called Yasudev and Devaki. When they married there was an evil king on the throne called Kans. Kans put Yasudev and Devaki into prison because a wise old man had predicted that their eighth child would kill King Kans. The first six children were killed by the evil king, but the seventh was smuggled out of prison and looked after by Yasudev's sister.

When the eighth child was due to be born, the king placed extra guards outside the prison cell. That night it rained heavily and there was thunder and lightening all around. After the child, Krishna, was born, the prison doors miraculously opened and all the guards were in a deep sleep. Yasudev carried the baby across the river and took him to safety in a friend's house.

Some stories go on to tell how King Kans sent an evil demon, Putna, to the village to kill the baby Krishna. Putna changed her form from a demon to beautiful young woman. She went to the village as a wet nurse, and when she fed Krishna from her breast it was filled with poison. But Krishna sucked out all the poison, which killed Putna. As she fell to the ground she returned to her ugly form as a demon. Krishna had survived, but the poison turned him blue.

Krishna's forms

The image of Krishna takes many different forms. Sometimes he is shown as a mischievous baby, or as a young child spilling the butter jar and eating some butter. He is also shown as a young man playing the flute. Although he was a mighty prince, he is often seen looking after cows. At times he is seen dancing with young milkmaids. Sometimes he is shown with his loved one, Radha, and sometimes he is a warrior and chariot driver (see pages 90 and 91).

1 Each of the different forms of Krishna tells us something about the way Hindus think of God. For example, the love that Radha had for Krishna is like the love that Hindus have for God. Write a sentence to show how each of the forms of Krishna tell us something about Hindu beliefs in God.

2 What does the story about Krishna teach us about fear, danger, good and evil, love, and God.

3 Read this quotation from one of the holy books:

'O Krishna, blessed indeed are they who but hear of Thee and meditate on thy divine life and thy divine play, for they become free from all worldly desires and attain to thy being. Thou art our beloved, Thou art our very self.' (Srimad Bhagavatam 2)

Copy this extract into your book and explain in your own words what it means.

Who was Krishna an avatar of?

For your dictionary 📖

The **Bhagavad Gita** ('the song of the Lord') is a collection of Krishna's words, and the most important scripture for many Hindus.

- Which king tried to kill the baby Krishna?
- Why did he want Krishna dead?
- Why does Krishna have blue skin?

Who is Rama?

Rama is the seventh avatar of Vishnu – he has a 'V' on his forehead to show this. Unusually, statues and pictures of Rama normally have only two arms (this shows that he was here on earth as a human) and he is always shown holding a bow and arrow (indicating his readiness to destroy evil). He represents the ideal man: strong, gallant and faithful to his one wife.

Rama is the hero of a great Indian story called the Ramayana (see pages 92 and 93). He saved the world from the evil, ten-headed King Ravana after many adventures in the forest.

A story from the Ramayana

Rama was in exile in the forest with his wife, **Sita**, and one of his brothers, Lakshmana. They all lived in a hut in the forest.

One day when he was out walking he met a young lady, Sarup Nakha, who was the evil King Ravana's sister. She tried to seduce him, so Rama had to use force to stop her intentions and according to some traditions he cut off her nose. Sarup Nakha went to her brother, the King, and pleaded with him to take revenge.

Ravana worked out a cunning plan. His servant, Marich, who could transform into other animals, changed into a deer and lured Rama into the forest on a hunting trip. Lakshmana was told to stay and protect Sita.

As Rama killed the deer, Marich shouted (and here he imitated Rama's voice) 'Lakshmana, come quick!' Lakshmana drew a protective circle around Sita's hut and told her not to set foot outside the circle. He then ran into the forest to help his brother.

Ravana, disguised as a holy man, went to the hut and asked Sita to bring him some food. Sita could not refuse. As she stepped out of the circle, Ravana threw off his disguise and captured Sita. You can read the last part of the story on pages 92 and 93.

Who were Lakshmana, Rama and Sita?

Why is Rama always shown carrying a bow and arrow?

For your dictionary

Sita is the female energy of Rama.

1 The Ramayana is a great story to act out or to perform as a puppet show.

a Design and make shadow puppet images of the characters in the story. You will need the warriors Rama and Lakshmana, the beautiful Sita, and Sarup Nakha (with detachable nose!). You will also need Marich as a deer and Ravana (both as an evil, ten-headed demon and also disguised as a holy man).

b In groups, perform the story so far.

2 a Sita was faced with a moral dilemma – should she step outside the circle? Did she do the right thing to endanger herself to help the holy man?

b Lakshmana also had a dilemma. What was it?

c Have you ever had a similar dilemma? Give an example of a time when you have been faced with a decision which meant disobeying someone even though you thought it was right to do so.

- Why does Rama carry a bow and arrow?
- Why does Rama have a 'V' sign on his forehead?
- Who is Rama's wife?

Look back

Avatar (page 13)
Rama (page 13)
Ramayana (page 13)
Vishnu (page 10)

Who is the Mother Goddess?

Most Hindus believe that the male gods have no power without the female goddesses. It is the male and the female together which causes energy – one is powerless without the other. With more than 200 million gods in Hinduism, there are an equal number of goddesses. On this page we shall look at just a few.

Each of the male gods has his own female goddess. Some of them are:

- **Saraswati** is the female energy of Brahma.
- **Lakshmi** is the female energy of Vishnu.
- Parvati is the female energy of Shiva.

Any goddess may be called the Mother Goddess. In Britain, she is usually worshipped as Ambe or **Durga**.

What is Lakshmi the goddess of?

Saraswati

As the goddess of music, craft and learning, Saraswati is often seen carrying a lute, a rosary (a string of prayer beads) and a book. In different parts of India she may have other musical instruments. She is usually seen with a peacock or a swan to symbolise the world in all its glory and wisdom.

Lakshmi

Lakshmi is the goddess of good luck. She is worshipped in Hindu homes throughout the year, but her special day is Divali (see pages 26 and 27). Each time that Vishnu has come to earth as an avatar, Lakshmi has come too. When Rama came she appeared as Sita, and when Krishna came she was his loved one, Radha. Hindus pray to Lakshmi when they want good fortune – both in marriage and in business. She is especially honoured by business people.

Durga

Durga is usually shown sitting on a lion. She has many arms and holds symbols of different gods in each hand. There are a number of stories as to how Durga came into being. One of them involves a demon buffalo. None of the gods could kill the buffalo, so they came together and put all their power into one form – Durga. She battled with the fearsome buffalo and eventually killed it. You will read more about Durga on pages 24 and 25.

Kali

Kali has received bad publicity in the West. Most people associate her as the goddess being worshipped in the story of *Indiana Jones and the Temple of Doom*, or being involved in human sacrifices. Her picture brings fear and dread to many people, but, despite being fierce, Kali has two sides. She represents 'power' or 'time'. Time is always passing and taking away our youth. She represents the awesome power of God – something not to be treated without fear. She is sometimes shown standing on Shiva, because one story tells how she got so carried away in killing a demon that she could not stop destroying. Shiva lay at her feet and when she trod on him she realised that she had to stop.

Which birds are usually associated with Saraswati?

- What differences can you see between Lakshmi and Saraswati?
- Who are Durga and Kali?
- Is the Mother Goddess gentle or fierce?

 Look back

Avatar (page 13)
Brahma (page 10)
Divali (page 5)
Krishna (page 13)
Parvati (page 15)
Rama (page 13)
Shiva (page 7)
Sita (page 19)
Vishnu (page 10)

For your dictionary

Durga is one form of the Mother Goddess.
Kali is a fearsome form of the Mother Goddess.
Lakshmi is Vishnu's wife. She is often shown holding a lotus flower.
Saraswati is the female energy (or 'consort') of Brahma.

1 From what you have read about the Mother Goddess, describe how you think Hindus picture the female side of God.

2 Why do you think Hinduism has many aspects of God, both male and female?

3 Female goddesses mentioned here symbolise good luck, wisdom, power, education, protection, music, crafts and beauty. Write a poem which mentions some of these virtues.

Ganesha?

..., a much loved God, is considered to be the son of Parvati
...iva. He is extremely important because before any worship
... be made to the gods, he must be worshipped first. He will
remove objects and problems that get in the way of real worship.
In fact, he is the God of beginnings. Before beginning anything
new, Hindus approach Ganesha and ask for his help to overcome
difficulties and obstacles.

A story about Ganesha

There are many stories about
Ganesha. This is just one of them.

Shiva was away from Parvati for
a long time, so Parvati became
very lonely. She took some mud
from the River Ganges and made
a model of a boy. That boy came
to life and she called him
Ganesha. When he was still
young she asked him to guard
the path to the river while she
went to bathe. Ganesha stood
guard in the centre of the path
with a sword.

Shiva returned home and, not
knowing who Ganesha was,
asked him where Parvati was.
Ganesha told him that she was
bathing in the river, so he could
not pass. Shiva laughed that
such a small boy should try to
stop him. As he went to pass,
Ganesha wielded his sword and
took a swipe at Shiva. This
angered Shiva, who drew his
own sword and sliced off the
young boy's head.

When he got to the river he
greeted Parvati, who asked
Shiva if he had seen their son on
the path to the river. Shiva was
horrified, and ordered his
servant, Nandi, to go to earth
and bring back the first head he
could find. Nandi brought back
an elephant's head and Shiva
put it on the shoulders of his son.

Ganesha was saved and he had
many adventures as one of
Shiva's sons. He is often shown
in pictures carrying his father's
trident, or with a snake around
his waist.

Why must Ganesha be worshipped before any other gods?

- Who is Shiva's consort?
- Why did Parvati make a son?
- How did Ganesha get an elephant's head?

For your dictionary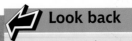

Ganesha was created by Parvati. He is the remover of obstacles and difficulties.

Look back

Parvati (page 15)
Shiva (page 7)

1 The following 11 words can be found across, down and diagonally in the wordsearch below.

a Copy the wordsearch carefully into your book. Then find each word, putting a circle around each one as you find it. The first one has been found for you.

b Some letters are left over. What word do they spell out?

Ganesha	Literal	God
Shiva	Parvati	Nandi
India	Hindu	Snake
Head	Path	

G	A	N	E	S	H	A
L	O	U	E	L	I	E
A	I	D	N	A	N	D
R	P	N	S	H	D	A
E	A	I	H	N	I	E
T	T	H	I	T	A	H
I	T	A	V	R	A	P
L	E	K	A	N	S	P

2 Read these two statements, which are both by Hindu people living in Britain today.

'Many young Hindus in Britain think of Ganesha as just an elephant-god, because they do not know all the stories about him. In India some of the films start with a picture of Ganesha, and many books have his picture on the first page. I think it is difficult for young people to discriminate between the cartoons they see on television and the gods. Cartoons have talking animals, but these are just to entertain us and make us laugh. Ganesha is much more than that; he is a great God with great power.'

'Of course Ganesha is a useful symbol of what God can do. When we have problems in our life, it is easy to picture God as an elephant. The elephant tears great tree trunks from the ground. If I have a problem, I want God to help me to tear down that problem from in front of me.'

a Write a paragraph to explain how their views differ.

b Which view could be described as symbolic and which could be described as literal? Give your reasons.

3 Copy this paragraph into your book and fill in the missing words as you go.

Hindus believe that _____ must be worshipped before they can worship any other god. They believe that he _____ obstacles and problems. He is worshipped to ensure good fortune. He is thought to be the son of _____ and _____. He gained an elephant's head when _____ cut off his human head. Some Hindus believe in him literally and others _____.

4 a Do you have anything to help you to overcome problems? Some people have lucky charms – do you?

b Write a letter describing the things you use to help you to overcome difficulties.

Festivals
What is Durga Puja?

Durga Puja is an annual Hindu festival in honour of the goddess Durga. It is a celebration of good over evil but different regions in India have their own customs. In some places they celebrate Durga as being on earth during the first nine nights and on the tenth day she returns to the heavens. The nine days are called **Navaratri** and the tenth day **Dassehra**.

Good over evil

Durga Puja is a great festival to show good triumphing over evil. There are many stories to show this, and here are two of them.

- All the gods were threatened by a demon called Mahisha, who had taken the shape of a buffalo. The gods could not kill the buffalo, so they went to Durga for help. The gods gave her all their weapons and all their strength. Durga attacked Mahisha, but Mahisha kept changing shape – from buffalo to lion to elephant and back to buffalo. As Durga cut Mahisha, black blood was spilled from the demon. As the blood touched the ground, so it changed into more demons which also attacked Durga. Durga fought bravely and eventually she stood on the buffalo and cut off his head with a sword.

- Rama has killed the evil demon Ravana, the king with ten heads. Each of his ten heads represents a different sin, so, during the period of Durga Puja, Hindus think about how they should live decently and without sin.

During Durga Puja, many Hindus tell the story of the Ramayana using puppets or models. During the ten days they tell the story in instalments and on the last day there will be a great fair and fireworks are let off.

Durga Puja in Britain

This is how one young Hindu described the festival:

'As people arrived, they washed their hands and took off their shoes. As I walked in, I heard music being played and I saw a group of musicians sitting on the floor near to the front. Children were wandering around and some were eating prashad. It was noisy and there were ghee lamps and incense burning. In the centre of the mandir was a **madh**.

For an hour or so people arrived and did their own worship to the gods. At about ten o'clock in the evening the priest brought a drum to the centre and he started to beat it in time with the music. The people started to sing, chant and clap their hands. Children collected some dandya [short sticks] and formed a circle around the madh. The priest led an arti service for ten minutes. This ended with everyone making a loud noise: bells were rung, drums were banged, sticks clicked together and a conch shell was blown. Some women joined the children in a circle around the madh and they all started to dance. The dance was a circle dance where everyone turned from the shrine, walked a couple of paces around the shrine and then turned back to face it again.

After about half an hour, the women sat down and the men formed a circle and repeated the same dance. Finally, they sat down and the women danced again, but this time the dance involved clashing the sticks with another person's sticks. As they danced everyone called Durga to 'come to us'. The dance is called Raas Garba. Eventually the dancing stopped and everyone went into another room where a meal was waiting. About a thousand people were fed. I am told that this service and meal is repeated every day of Navaratri.'

- Why is Durga Puja celebrated?
- What is a dandya?
- Who is Mahisha?

What is a madh?

For your dictionary

Dassehra, meaning 'ten days', celebrates the end of Durga Puja.
Durga Puja is an important Hindu festival in honour of the goddess Durga to celebrate good triumphing over evil.
A **madh** is a cylindrical shrine placed in the centre of the room with images of Durga facing outwards.
Navaratri, meaning 'nine nights', is the festival which happens as part of Durga Puja in honour of the goddess.

 Look back

Arti (page 9)
Durga (page 21)
Ghee (page 9)
Mandir (page 9)
Prashad (page 9)
Rama (page 13)
Ramayana (page 13)

1 Many Hindus see the story of Durga fighting Mahisha as a parable (a story with an important message). What do you think the message of the story is?

2 How many days does Durga Puja last each year?

3 Imagine that you were in the mandir during the festivities. Write a letter to a friend describing what you saw.

4 Make two dandya. They are about 40cm long and highly decorated. Some have bells on the end.

What is Divali?

Divali, the festival of lights, is celebrated throughout India and wherever there are Hindus in the world. It is sometimes called Deepawalee, Deepawali or Diwali. It can last as long as five days but there are two main days of celebration.

This is how one young Hindu described the festival:

Why do people send each other Divali cards?

Day 1

We cleaned and tidied our house so that it was perfect for Lakshmi to visit us. My mum prepared special party food whilst my big sister made a **rangoli** out of coloured rice outside the back door. It was my job to get a **diva lamp** ready in the front window.

When evening came we went to the mandir. My dad took his account books and completed the year's accounts in front of the **murti** of Lakshmi.

The mandir was very full and everyone brought a candle or diva lamp and lit it in front of the murti. Before the evening **puja** to Lakshmi had finished, we children ran outside so we could get a good position for the fireworks.

After the fireworks we went home, eating the sweets that we got for prashad. The sweets were very rich and you could not eat more than two of them without feeling sick! When we got home we were told to go to sleep quickly and then Lakshmi would visit our house. We were told that if we had been naughty during the year she might not visit.

Day 2

When I woke up in the morning there were presents — new clothes, sweets and some money.

The second day is New Year's Day. After morning puja, my father's brother came over with his family. The telephone seemed to ring every few minutes with someone wishing us a Happy New Year.

We all went into town and visited the fair. Most of the money that we got was spent on the rides. Divali cards decorated all the shops and there were special Divali bargains. My dad bought my mum some new gold jewellery as a present.

In the evening we all went home and ate a special meal. Everyone stayed up very late and we all played games and talked.

Look back

Divali (page 5)
Ghee (page 9)
Lakshmi (page 21)
Mandir (page 9)
Prashad (page 9)

For your dictionary

A **diva lamp** is a lamp which burns ghee.

A **murti** is any image used as a focus of worship.

Puja is an act of worship carried out by Hindus in a mandir or at home.

Rangolis are circular pictures which are drawn with chalks or made from coloured rice. A typical design shows a circular border containing a square, which is divided into four triangles.

- What preparations do Hindus make to get ready for Divali?
- What is a rangoli?
- What is Divali the festival of?

Why are lamps lit at this time?

1 Lakshmi brings good fortune if you have been good. Suggest two reasons why Hindu business people may choose to finish their accounts in front of Lakshmi.

2 Design your own rangoli using as many colours as you like. Use food colouring to colour the rice.

3 Imagine that you keep a diary. Write an entry in your diary for each of the two days of Divali mentioned on these pages. Do not forget to write about your thoughts as well as the details of the day.

What is Holi?

The festival of **Holi** is in the spring. The celebrations can carry on for many days but there are two main days: Holi and Holikah Dal. Often the festival is called the 'grand festival of colours'. There are many stories connected to the celebrations. Holi is a time when people break away from routine and have fun.

A Holi story

A king had a son, Prahlad, and a daughter, Holika. Prahlad was devoted to God and prayed all the time. His father forbade him to pray but Prahlad would not stop. The king ordered Holika to carry Prahlad into a fire and sit him upon her lap – everyone thought that Holika could not be killed by fire. When the flames died away, Prahlad, who had been saved, stepped out of the fire, but Holika had been burnt to death.

What happens at Holi?

Holi is a fun festival, when everyone can really relax and enjoy themselves. People spring-clean their houses and throw out all their winter rubbish. It is a time of practical jokes; everyone wears old clothes and people of all ages join in the fun at throwing coloured water and chalk at each other.

A big bonfire is lit to remind Hindus of Prahlad. Sometimes models of Holika are made and thrown into the fire, and coconuts are cooked on the bonfire and eaten.

Symbols of Holi

One story tells of Krishna having a water-fight with young milkmaids, so the coloured water symbolises his joy of life. In another story the water represents the blood that was spilled when Krishna killed an evil demon. The bonfire symbolises the test for that which is good and that which is evil. Dancing is connected with the pleasure that spring has come and the crops will soon start to grow.

Dancing during the Holi festival. What are the different days of the festival called?

- What is the meaning of the story about Prahlad and Holika?
- Why was Prahlad sent to be burnt in the fire?
- Why do people throw coloured water at each other during Holi?

For your dictionary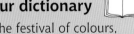

Holi is the festival of colours, celebrated in the spring.

Look back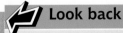

Krishna (page 13)

1 Complete the following sentences by matching the beginnings on the left with the correct ending from the list on the right.

Holi is sometimes called	of the struggle between good and evil
When Holika took Prahlad into the fire	of Krishna's high spirits and sense of fun
Coloured water is thrown as a reminder	Prahlad was saved but she died
The bonfire is a symbol	the grand festival of colours

2 Imagine that you are going to organise a procession for Holi. Write a letter to the local police telling them about the festival and what will happen.

3 Design and make a poster advertising the events during Holi.

What is Raksha Bandhan?

Raksha Bandhan is a festival where brothers and sisters show their love and affection for each other. On this day women and girls tie a bracelet around their brothers' right wrists. This bracelet is called a **rakhi** and it acts as a lucky charm for the next year. It is traditional for the brother to give his sisters presents such as money, sweets, fruit, or a sari.

Brothers and sisters

Traditionally, Hindu family life is very close and protective. A Hindu boy may take on the role of protector of his sister and of her honour. She cares for him and feeds him, and he ensures that no harm comes her way. Raksha Bandhan celebrates this special relationship.

If their parents die, 'the brothers should individually give their unmarried sisters something from their own wealth, a quarter share of their own wealth. If they did not give this they would fall.' *(Laws of Manu 9:118)*

What is happening in this picture?

Origins

The story tells of Indra, the Lord of Heaven, who fought and lost in a battle against some demons. He prepared himself to fight once more, but before he left his wife, Sachi, tied a holy thread around his wrist. Indra fought and defeated the demons because he was protected by the bracelet.

Protection

As rakhis are a symbol of mutual love and protection, priests also tie them around the wrists of worshippers. A **mantra** is read, which is believed to help protect the wearer of the bracelet from evil:

'Yena baddho balee raajaa daanavendro mahaabalah: Tena twaam anuubadhnaami rakshey maa chala maa chala.'

In return, the priest is given presents or money.

Nowadays, some people tie rakhis on close friends, and as a symbol of friendship at weddings.

For your dictionary

A **mantra** is a short verse of scripture or prayer which is repeated or chanted.
A **rakhi** is a bracelet, usually made out of silk or cotton, tied to give protection and strengthen friendship and love.
Raksha Bandhan is the festival when girls tie a decorative bracelet (rakhi) around their brothers' wrists.

- Who gave Indra a rakhi?
- When might a rakhi be given nowadays?
- Why is a rakhi worn?

---

1 Write a letter to a friend describing how you think brothers and sisters should look after each other.

2 Make a rakhi like this.

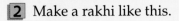

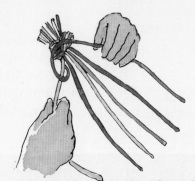

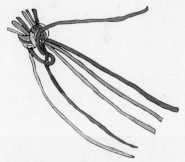

a Take six pieces of coloured wool about 25cm long, and tie all six pieces together at one end.

b Take the two lengths of wool on the left and tie them tightly in a single knot next to the main knot.

c Knot the second piece of wool tightly with the third, the third with the fourth, and so on. Start again from the left when you have done one row.

d Keep knotting until you have your required length. All knots should be even – if your first attempt does not look too good, you will get better with practice!

3 How might wearing a rakhi help someone?

4 In what situations would you most need a good-luck charm?

What are the other festivals?

There are too many Hindu festivals to show in one book. All the gods have days when they are remembered and worshipped. Many of the festivals have connections with the seasons, while others are connected to the cycle of the moon. On pages 24 to 31 we have looked at some of the most widely celebrated festivals. Here we shall look at a few of the others.

Some festivals take place once every few years, but most happen at the same time each year. Some gods are celebrated by the worshippers of just that particular god, while others are celebrated by all Hindus.

Main Hindu festivals

January	Makar Sankrant (**Pongal**)
February	Saraswati Puja (**Vasanta Panchami**)
March	Birthday of Sri Ramakrishna
	Shivarati (Shiva night)
	Holi
April	Birthday of Lord Rama
August	Raksha Bandhan
	Birthday of Lord Krishna
September	Birthday of Ganesha
October	Durga Puja
End Oct–Beg Nov	Divali
December	Birthday of the Gita
	Vaikunta Ekadashi (fast for Vishnu)

The Hindu calendar has twelve months in a year, but the months do not fit easily into the British calendar. The official New Year festival is in March or April, but New Year is celebrated at other times of year as well.

Fasting

Hindu people may **fast** twice a month and many will try to fast during Vaikunta Ekadashi. This is a special day when worshippers think of Vishnu. Some Hindus will try to spend the day without drinking even a sip of water, but most will have a little water but no rice. People who find fasting difficult may eat a little fruit and drink some milk.

Hindus have different reasons for fasting. For some people it is to purify the body and the mind; others fast simply because the holy scriptures tell them to; and some fast because it helps them to practice self-control: a day without food helps them to think about how much they might take food for granted.

- In which month is the birthday of Ganesha celebrated?
- Why do Hindus fast?
- During which festival do Hindus stay awake all night?

Look back

Divali (page 5)
Durga Puja (page 25)
Ganesha (page 23)
Holi (page 29)
Krishna (page 13)
Mandir (page 9)
Raksha Bandhan (page 31)
Rama (page 13)
Shiva (page 7)
Vishnu (page 10)

Rice being offered to the gods at Pongal. When is Pongal celebrated?

Which festival might this be? Which gods are being worshipped?

Shivarati

On Shivarati, Hindus spend the day fasting before going to the mandir for the whole night. During the night they wash the Shiva linga every three hours. They pour milk, curd, honey, rosewater and water over the linga. Songs are sung and people walk around the linga from time to time. They say the following prayer:

'O Lord! I will bathe Thee with water, milk, curd and honey. Do thou kindly bathe me with wisdom. Do thou kindly wash away my sins.'

For your dictionary

To **fast** is to go without food or drink.
Corn is harvested at the **Pongal** festival. To some Hindus this is New Year's Day.
Vasanta Panchami is the first day of spring in the Hindu calendar. Hindus bathe, worship the sun and the River Ganges, and dress in yellow.

1 Draw a large circle on a clean piece of paper. Divide the circle evenly into twelve segments, and label the segments with the months of the year.
a Using one colour, plot the names of the three main festivals – Durga Puja, Divali and Holi.
b Using another colour, plot all the birthdays.
c In a third colour, plot all the other festivals.

2 Write a paragraph called 'Why Hindus fast'.

3 Copy the Shivarati prayer and draw pictures to illustrate it. In your own words, explain what the prayer means.

What is arti?

The word 'arti' means 'light' or 'flame'. The arti service normally takes place at sunrise and sunset, but some Hindus perform arti at other times as well. Many Hindus perform arti at home but some also go to the mandir for daily arti services.

In the mandir

Hindus stand in front of the murti in the mandir. The priest walks to the front, and begins to chant the arti prayer. The people join in. While the prayer is being chanted, bells are rung, gongs banged, hands clapped, cymbals clashed and a conch shell may be blown. During the 15 minutes the service takes, the priest may wave a brush made of yak hair and rotate the tray containing the arti lamps in front of the murti. At the end of the prayer, the priest comes up to each of the people there and offers them the lamp. Worshippers place some money on the tray and warm their hands on the lamp. As they leave they are offered prashad.

Prashad

Prashad means 'the food of the gods'. It can take the form of a piece of fruit, a sweet or even a complete meal, but is usually a sweet made of sugar, water, ghee and semolina.

On certain days, British Hindu families work together to provide a meal for all the people at the mandir – sometimes more than a thousand people. On special festivals the whole temple committee may work together to feed even larger crowds. A typical meal would be 'Vegetable Thali': a number of different vegetable dishes such as bombay potato, chana dahl, raita, rice, bhagee, and possibly a sweet made from butter.

Why might this priest be holding a conch shell?

Recipe for prashad

1 cup sugar

2 cups water

1 cup ghee

1 cup semolina

Dissolve the sugar in the water and bring to the boil. Remove from the heat. Cook the ghee and semolina in a pan until the mixture is golden-brown. Stir all the time so that it does not burn. Add the sugar and water mixture and stir. When all the liquid has been absorbed, your prashad is ready. It is best eaten warm, but is also good cold.

How is the arti lamp used?

- What does the word 'arti' mean?
- What do you think the arti lamp represents?
- What does 'prashad' mean?

 Look back

Arti (page 9)
Ghee (page 9)
Mandir (page 9)
Murti (page 27)
Prashad (page 9)

1 This is part of prayer which is read at every arti service:

'Hail to thee, O lord of the universe,
Remover of sorrows and master of all
Salutations and prostrations unto thee.
O instant remover of the troubles of the devotees,
Thou rewardest those who sing Thy glories and removest their sorrow.
With Thy Name happiness and prosperity dawn, and pain disappears...
Thou art protector of all...
Thou art only one and still invisible,
O merciful God! Guide ignorant beings to thy divine knowledge.'

Copy the line which most appeals to you and say why you chose those words.

2 Why do you think that some Hindus chant the arti prayer several times during the day?

3 Write a phrase or a saying that you could recite every day which would help you to remember what is important to you.

4 Create a recipe of your own which would be suitable for prashad.

What is the havan?

The **havan** is the holy fire. The service is sometimes called yajna, which is a **sanskrit** word for sacrifice. The havan is used at weddings, puja and special Shiva festivals. Making offerings into a fire is an old custom, written about in the Vedas, which is linked to the ancient ritual of the bride taking a fire into her husband's home and tending it as long as she lives.

Fire in ancient Hinduism

In the distant past, fire was difficult to start, hard to control and very powerful. Fire became very important to the Aryans because they used it to make bronze weapons. Fire was also important because of its link with the sun.

In the Vedas we read that Hindus had to allow milk to boil over into the fire as a sacrifice. If they did not, there was a fear that the sun would not rise. The Vedas also describe other sacrifices where ghee was poured into the fire, then an animal was sacrificed, and finally more ghee was added:

'An offering cast properly into the fire approaches the sun.' (Laws of Manu 3:76)

At the end of the service, water is sprinkled to put the fire out:

'When the whole series of rituals into the fire is finished... he should sprinkle some water on the ground with his right hand.' (Laws of Manu 3:214)

Agni

The Rig Veda contains many references to sacrifice, and Agni, the God of fire, is mentioned in it a great deal. Agni is often shown with two heads and six hands, and around his heads are tongues of fire. He lives on earth among humans and is found in every household. He is very powerful – without him humans could not survive.

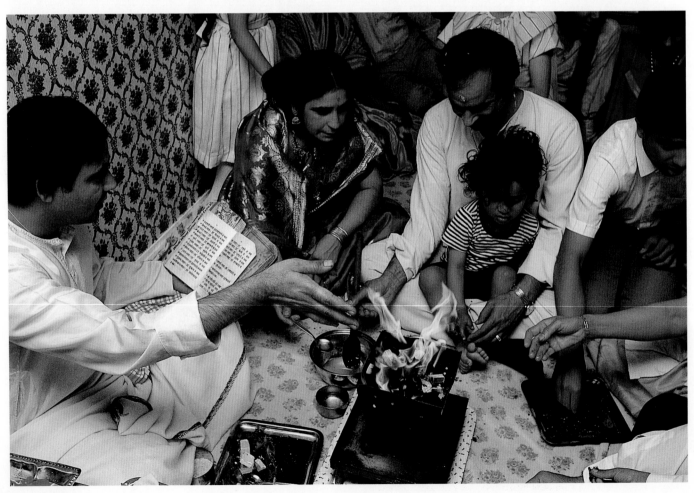

What happens during the havan ceremony?

What is Agni the god of?

- What is the connection between the havan and the sun?
- Why is fire used in havan services?
- Who is the God of fire?

1 This is a description of a havan ceremony:

'It was at 10.00 a.m. that I was told to sit at the front of the mandir with the family who were about to have puja. There was a metal furnace standing on some bricks and this was already alight with burning wood. Words were chanted by the priest and various things were thrown into the fire. This included ghee, grain and herbs. A man went around the people with a tray, and those who were too far from the fire to throw in their offerings placed them on it. Then the tray was brought to the front and the offerings were poured in.

At times the fire grew fierce. More wood and ghee were added to the fire. The priest used a spoon to pour more liquid into the fire, and then the back of the spoon was placed on the centre of each of our foreheads. At the end of the service, the priest gave each of us a sweet.'

Draw a series of pictures to describe the havan service.

2 In this crossword you have the answers but the clues are missing. Make up your own short clues to go with each answer.

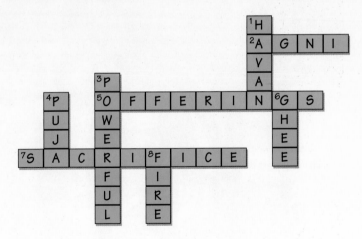

3 Many ancient people treated fire as a god. Write a paragraph to explain why.

4 Why might people have thought that the sun needed a sacrifice?

For your dictionary 📖

Havan is a form of worship where ghee and grain are offered into a fire.
Sanskrit is the ancient language in which many of the Hindu holy books were written.

Look back

Aryans (page 7)
Ghee (page 9)
Mandir (page 9)
Puja (page 27)
Rig Veda (page 7)
Shiva (page 7)
Vedas (page 15)

What is puja?

The word puja means 'worship' and this can take place either at home or in the mandir. Some Hindus perform puja every day; others less often. Everyday puja usually involves making offerings to a god and reciting mantras, but for special occasions – such as giving thanks to God for a new baby, in memory of a loved one or to celebrate a wedding anniversary – families may ask the priest to perform a special puja.

A typical puja might follow this pattern:

The family sit in front of the murti, with a priest. They bring various offerings including milk, flower petals, yoghurt, ghee, and even clothes. A little water is poured over each person's hands to symbolise purity (all the worshippers would have bathed and put on clean clothes before coming). Each person puts their finger into a special paste, placing a spot on Ganesha's forehead, and then on their own. The priest starts to chant in sanskrit. A small amount of water is offered to Ganesha, and some of the water is poured into the hands of the family and drunk. Seven spoonfuls of water are poured over Ganesha's head.

Next, the offerings are poured over the murti. Some of this liquid ('nectar') is collected in a small container and may be offered around to be drunk. Ganesha is then placed on a plate of coloured rice and a small **sacred thread** is placed around him. A red mark is placed on his forehead, and more flower petals and rice are offered to him. A bell is rung, incense and the ghee lamp are rotated, and food and sweets are offered to Ganesha. Mantras are chanted and songs may be sung.

This is just the first part of puja. Ganesha is worshipped before any other god, so this whole sequence may be repeated to another god. This is often done behind closed curtains – to protect the modesty of the god or goddess. At the end of the puja, the curtains are opened and everyone cheers and sings. Before leaving, prashad will be eaten.

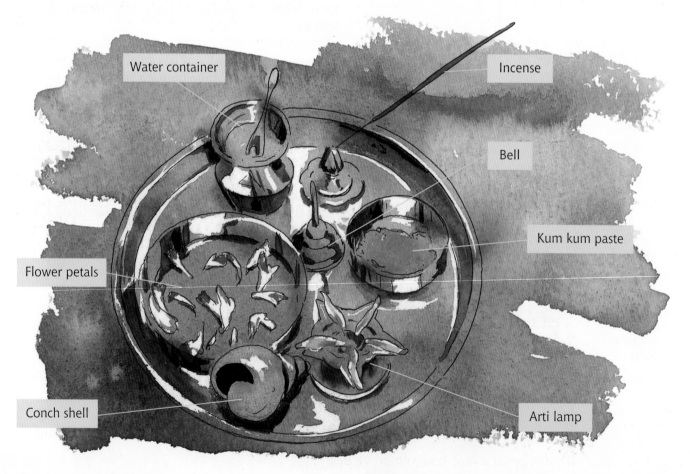

Water container

Incense

Bell

Kum kum paste

Flower petals

Conch shell

Arti lamp

How is a puja tray used?

Look back

Ganesha (page 23)
Ghee (page 9)
Krishna (page 13)
Mandir (page 9)
Mantra (page 31)
Murti (page 27)
Prashad (page 9)
Puja (page 27)
Sanskrit (page 37)
Shiva (page 7)

For your dictionary

Mala is a string of beads made of wood or dried seeds and used to help prayer.
A **sacred thread** is worn by Hindu males from the left shoulder to the right hip.

- Which god is worshipped before any other?
- Why is puja sometimes performed behind closed curtains?
- What does puja mean?

1 Read these two descriptions of puja.

One man came in and spent most of his time meditating, cross-legged. Another took milk to the Shiva linga, pouring it over it as he chanted. Another wandered around the mandir, quietly using his **mala** and chanting mantras. Another person sat with his eyes shut and his hands moving around him. Others simply rushed in, put some money into a box in front of the gods, and then sat in the middle of the mandir for a while. Some kneeled in front of the murti and placed their foreheads on the ground. I even saw one person laying flat on the ground in front of the murti.

One of my friends said that puja is like playing with dolls. I think she expected me to get upset. I agreed with her. When you play with dolls, that doll becomes alive to you. You talk to it and you enjoy its company. When I take part in puja, I know the murti does not move but it does come alive to me. I can talk to it. God becomes alive to me – I talk to Krishna.

a Many different forms of worship are described here. Why do you think people worship in different ways?
b How does puja differ from any other worship you have seen or experienced?
c What does the word 'worship' mean to each of the people speaking here?

2 Each of the actions in puja is symbolic. Can you work out what some of them represent?

3 Draw your own picture of a puja tray and add labels to it.

How do Hindus worship at home?

A Hindu need never go to a mandir because a home is a temple. Fire is taken into the home when the wife comes to live with her husband. That fire is tended to and offered to the gods by the women in the family.

The role of women

The woman plays a very important role in worship at home. In the morning, she takes care of the family shrine, performs puja, and offers some of the family breakfast to God. Some of the food is then taken back into the kitchen and mixed with the food that the family will eat.

In many Hindu households, women pray at least three times a day, and at the end of the day a curtain is drawn around the murti so that it can rest.

The shrine

In almost every Hindu home there is a shrine containing small images of gods and goddesses. Framed pictures of deities may also be seen. The shrine is treated as a very holy place and is sometimes a whole room or sometimes just a small area is set aside for worship.

A Hindu prayer

Om
Resplendent Savita [the sun]
Let us meditate on the excellent
  splendour
Of the the god Savitri
May he stir our thoughts.

This is the most popular prayer at puja. It is called the **Gayatri Mantra**, and the words come from 'gaya' meaning to sing, 'tri' meaning three, and 'mantra' meaning prayer. So it is a prayer which should be sung three times a day. If Hindus recite this prayer sincerely it leads them to Right Action, Right Thought and Right Speech.

Why is food offered to the murti?

Look back

Deity (page 5)
Mandir (page 9)
Mantra (page 31)
Murti (page 27)
Puja (page 27)
Rig Veda (page 7)

For your dictionary

The **Gayatri Mantra** is the most sacred verse of the Rig Veda.

- What role do women play in worship at home?
- How must food be prepared?
- What does Gayatri Mantra mean?

1 Read this statement about food by a young Hindu:

'Food is very important in our house. We must make all our food with calm thoughts. We offer the food to the murti because it will then be blessed. The eating of the food will then make us all blessed. I suppose we could say, 'you are what you eat.'

Why is food blessed before being eaten?

2 Copy the Gayatri Mantra and draw a picture to show what it means.

3 The Gayatri Mantra refers to Right Action, Right Thought and Right Speech. Give examples to show what you think these three things mean.

4 Most Hindus do not *have* to perform puja, so why do you think most are happy to do so?

5 It has been said that 'a home without a murti is not a home – it is just a building'. Explain in your own words what this means.

41

How do Hindus worship in a mandir in Britain?

The Hindu word for temple is 'mandir'. As we have seen on pages 40 to 41, worship can take place at home but here we will look at some of the community temples found in Britain.

Visting a mandir

- Make sure that you are clean and that your clothes are suitable (roll down sleeves and cover legs).
- Wash your hands and take off your shoes before entering.
- Hindus may ring a bell as they enter the shrine-room.
- Do not stand between a worshipper and the murti, but you may sit on the floor with other worshippers.
- In some mandirs, men and women sit in separate places.
- Do not touch the murti.
- On your way out take any prashad that is offered, and treat it with respect.
- If you can, give some money at the end of your visit.
- Write a letter to thank them for the visit.

How can you tell that this mandir is in Britain?

This is the new mandir in Neasdon, London. How does it differ from other British buildings?

Hindus do not need to go to the mandir very often, but many will try to go once a week. When they get there, they may offer money, milk and fruit to the murti; they may just sit and watch what is going on; or they may take part in puja or arti. Some people play musical instruments, others may chant or sing, and some may have come for a special personal ceremony.

Purpose-built mandirs

Mandirs in Britain are sometimes converted houses or churches, but there are also special purpose-built buildings.

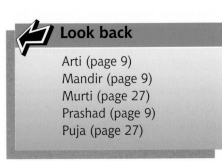

Look back

Arti (page 9)
Mandir (page 9)
Murti (page 27)
Prashad (page 9)
Puja (page 27)

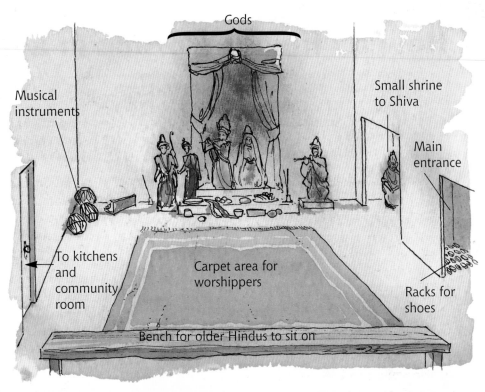

What happens at each of the places shown on this plan of a typical mandir?

- What is the Hindu word for temple?
- What must you do before you enter a mandir?
- What do Hindus do in a mandir?

1 Read these ten statements carefully. Copy the true statements into your book, and correct the wrong ones before writing them out.
a When entering a mandir, make sure that you take off your shoes.
b Wash your feet before entering a mandir.
c Wear old clothes to a mandir, because you will be sitting on the floor.
d Hindus may sound a horn as they enter the shrine-room.
e Do not touch the murti.
f All Hindus do not do the same things when they are in a mandir.
g Hindus will offer food and money to the gods.
h Hindus sit on chairs in the shrine-room.
i You should take some prashad if it is offered to you.
j Hindus do not make any sound in a mandir.

2 This page on the right is taken from a mandir notice-board. Write a newspaper report or design a poster to show all the different activities that go on there.

Every day
10.00 a.m. to 12.00 noon,
4.00 p.m. to 10.00 p.m.
    Library open
4.00 p.m. to 5.00 p.m.
    Lessons in Hindi for children
5.00 p.m. to 5.30 p.m.
    Dance group
9.00 p.m. Prashad.
Friday
7.30 p.m. to 10.00 p.m.
    Youth club
Saturday
10.00 a.m. to 12.00 noon
    Morning school
2.00 p.m. to 4.00 p.m.
    Film show
7.00 p.m. to 9.00 p.m.
    Youth discussion group
Sunday
Full religious programme.

How do Hindus worship in a mandir in India?

In India, wherever you look there are Hindu mandirs. Some are very large; others are just shelters beside the road for the murti. A mandir is the most colourful sight in the village. Many are built so that the murti will be facing towards the rising sun.

There are several important differences between mandirs in Britain and mandirs in India:

- Mandirs in India are often designed so that the wind can circulate in the building and cool everyone down.

- Many Indian mandirs are devoted to just one God and contain just one murti; mandirs in Britain often have many murti in them and are devoted to many gods.

- Most mandirs in Britain are made out of brick and look like ordinary British buildings. Many are converted halls and houses. Most mandirs in India are purpose-built, made out of marble and decorated around the outside with statues and paintings.

Even in India mandirs come in different designs. For example, near the Himalayas the roofs are made of wood and steeply sloped; in the rainy areas the roofs are made of tiles and sloped.

If you were to visit this mandir, you would remove your shoes and walk up some steps and under a carved arch. As you walked inside, you would see the murti directly in front of you – they are at the far end of the building under a pyramid-shaped tower. You would not be permitted to get too close to the murti, but you might be able to walk around them. If you want to take photographs, always ask permission beforehand and make sure you do not get in the way.

You would smell incense and ghee burning. There might be many people inside and it could be noisy. Some money could be donated to the God before leaving, and on your way out you would be given prashad.

- Why are temples in India different to most of those in Britain?
- Why is incense burned in mandirs?
- What is paisley a symbol of?

How do mandirs in India differ from region to region?

Symbols found in an Indian mandir

Many or all of these symbols may be found in Indian mandirs:

The swastika is a symbol of good luck, and it is usually drawn in red and used in decorative floor designs.

Paisley, a symbol of good luck, is now a common pattern in Britain.

The world was created out of a lotus flower. Goddesses are often seen standing on a lotus.

This is the symbol of om, the sound of God.

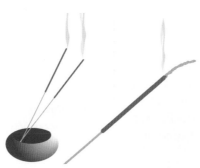

Incense is burned to sweeten the air.

Coconuts are thought to be the perfect food. They contain milk inside.

Diva lamps are lit to offer light to the gods and to the people.

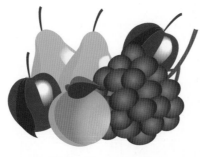

Fruit is offered to the gods.

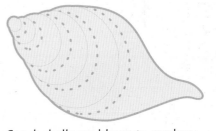

Conch shells are blown to awaken the gods.

Look back

Diva lamp (page 27)
Ghee (page 9)
Mandir (page 9)
Murti (page 27)
Om (page 5)
Prashad (page 9)

1 Write the following sentences in the correct order to make a paragraph about visiting an Indian mandir.

You smell ghee and incense.
You climb up some steps.
You take off your shoes.
You can walk around the murti
The murti is directly in front of you.
You will be given prashad as you leave.
The murti is under a pyramid-shaped tower.
The atmosphere inside the mandir is very noisy.
You give a donation to the murti.

2 Draw and label a picture of a shrine. Include all the symbols above.

How do Hindus worship in villages in India?

Many Hindus live in villages in India and their religion is an important part of their lives. Village life is very different to the life Hindus lead in the big cities or in Britain.

Village life

Traditionally, the villages were divided into sections so that people from the same caste lived near each other. Each caste was separate from the others, but people did help villagers from other castes. The villagers would not have used money in the past, so they relied upon everyone doing their own job so that the whole village could survive.

The brahmins probably live in one part of the village, the washer-people in another (usually near to the river), and the craftspeople somewhere else in the village. There are so many village traditions that it is impossible to mention them all. Some of them go back thousands of years, and all of them are important to the families who keep them. Many Hindus have left the villages and have gone to the cities, leaving these traditions behind.

Beliefs and customs

Villagers believe that God is all around them and everything has a religious meaning. They get up very early in the morning – before daylight. They bathe in the river and offer puja to rising sun. They take some water home to pour over their plants, and they make an offering to the deities in their houses. Next, they make a religious sign on their foreheads and then sit and meditate using mala beads. In the evening they pray and meditate to welcome in the evening.

Villagers have many customs. Some of them are:

- The right foot leaves the house before the left;
- Food is eaten from the right hand, not the left;
- When someone leaves to go on a journey, the room is not swept for a while because sweeping would make the person's journey unsuccessful;
- When someone leaves they should not be called back;
- Seeing a spider means that you will come into money.

Traditionally, farmers harvest their crops and give some to their teacher and some to the brahmins. They also give food to others in the village, such as the carpenter, the fishmonger, and the oil presser.

There is at least one mandir in the village. Many Hindu women take their cooked food to the mandir to offer some to God before taking it home for the family to eat.

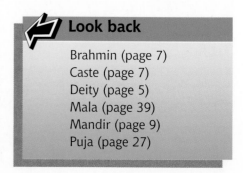

Look back

Brahmin (page 7)
Caste (page 7)
Deity (page 5)
Mala (page 39)
Mandir (page 9)
Puja (page 27)

Map labels: River, Harijans, Ghats, Brahmins, Washer men, Temple, Bridge keeper's house, School, Craftsmen, Small road, Farmers, Main road, Fields for crops, Fields for crops

Who lives closest to the school? Why do you think this is?

Would this farmer keep all his crops for himself?

- What is the first thing Hindu villagers do in the mornings?
- Where do Hindu women take their food before it is eaten?
- Why do the brahmins live nearest the school?

1 Read this quotation by a Hindu man:

'We did not really think of these traditions as our religion. It was our way of life. There was no difference between our religion and our lives – they were one and the same. Is it religious to eat from your right hand? Is it religious to light a lamp and place it in front of your house? We did it because we had always done it. These things only became religious when we moved to Britain. Then we noticed that not everyone did these things.'

In what way did this man's view of tradition change when he moved to Britain?

2 a Each family has its own customs and practices. List three things that your family does that you think are unique to you.
b Discuss in groups your answer to the above question. What sort of things are done differently? What things are done the same?

From birth to death
What are the samskaras and ashramas?

Most people celebrate or show respect for important times in their lives, such as birthdays and weddings. Hindus call these stages of life **samskaras**. There are up to 16 samskaras in a Hindu's life, and some of them are mentioned here.

Journey through life

Many Hindus see life as a journey. As they travel through life, they have to be careful to choose the correct roads and to be careful not to collect any bad karma. Each samskara helps them with this journey.

Ashramas

Hindus also believe that there are four **ashramas** in life:

- Brahmacharya (student);
- Grihastha (householder);
- Vanaparastha (retired);
- Sannyasa (holy person).

Traditionally, these ashramas were for men only, and women had to work and support men in all things. Today, however, many Hindu women are students, equal partners at home, teachers and holy people.

The soul travels through each stage, and it is important that Hindus live according to their position in life and the duties expected of them. This is called **varna-ashrama-dharma**.

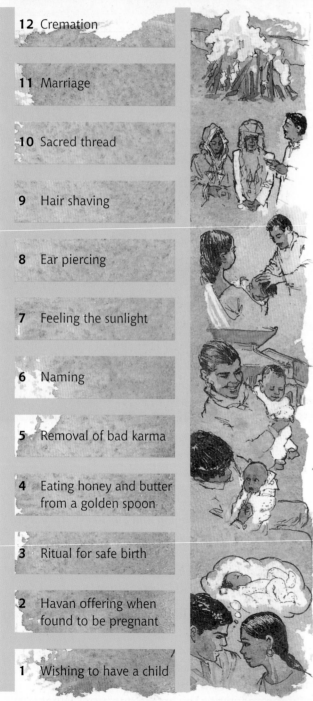

12 Cremation

11 Marriage

10 Sacred thread

9 Hair shaving

8 Ear piercing

7 Feeling the sunlight

6 Naming

5 Removal of bad karma

4 Eating honey and butter from a golden spoon

3 Ritual for safe birth

2 Havan offering when found to be pregnant

1 Wishing to have a child

For your dictionary

An **ashrama** is one of the four stages of life – student, householder, retired and spiritual pilgrim.
A **samskara** is a ritual to mark a new stage of life – not to be confused with samsara, the word to explain the cycle of birth, life, death, reincarnation.
Varna-ashrama-dharma refers to the duties of a way of life based on varna (social class), ashrama (a particular stage in life) and dharma (duty). It means that it is your duty to behave according to your position in life and which ashrama you have reached.

- What is a samskara?
- What is the first ashrama?
- What is the Hindu name for a holy man?

This diagram shows the samskaras as a ladder. Why are they shown like this?

Student

'He should avoid honey, meat, perfume, garlands, spices,... anything that has gone sour and violence.' (Laws of Manu 2:177)

Other things to be avoided are gossip, greed, putting on makeup, playing music, dancing, singing, looking at or touching women.

Householder

Most Hindus do not go beyond this ashrama – they look after their families until they die. This stage is the most important because it is the householder who has to work hard to ensure that the other three ashramas have all the food and shelter they need. In many countries, if you do not work, you have no way of surviving.

Retired

When a Hindu man retires from daily work, he may spend the rest of his life learning more about his religion and studying his favourite holy books. He is highly respected, and may be called upon to give advice. In India, he may leave the family home to live alone in the forest.

Holy man

A holy man gives up most material things, and meditates on the mysteries of life, death and rebirth. He has few belongings and begs for food.

 Look back

Havan (page 37)
Karma (page 7)
Reincarnation (page 5)
Sacred thread (page 39)

1 a There are various samskaras in different Hindu communities. Why do you think this is the case?
b Why are the main samskaras of birth, marriage and death the same among all Hindus?

2 What are the most important stages in your life? Some people choose things such as learning to walk and starting school. Make a list of twelve important stages in your life.

3 a Why are students advised to avoid certain things?
b Do you think students everywhere can follow these rules? Explain your answer.

What happens when a Hindu is born?

Having a new baby brings many changes at home. In Hinduism there are a number of samskaras to welcome the child into the world. Most of the rituals described on these pages were once only carried out on boys. However, in modern times, many girls undergo the same rituals as boys.

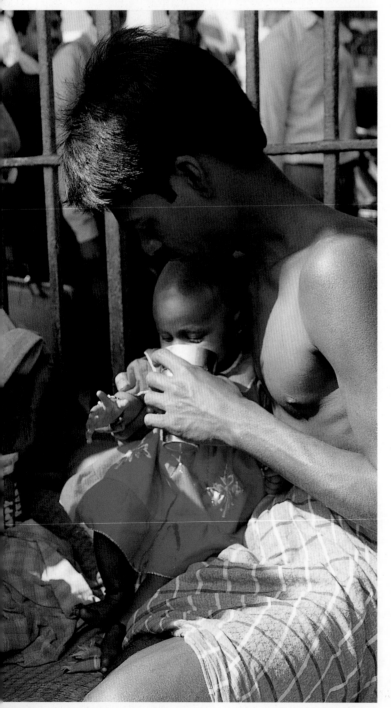

Naming

When a baby is born, the priest studies a horoscope to find out exactly where the planets were at the time of birth. From this he can work out which letter the child's name should begin with. He also highlights certain dates which will be special for the child.

A child's name is very important. He or she may be named after a god, a flower, a planet or even a mood. For example, the name 'Anand' means happy, and 'Gopal' is another name for Krishna.

Feeling the sunlight

The first journey out of the house officially takes place when the baby is three or four months old. Everyone bathes early and the father performs puja at home. The baby wears new clothes and has a spot marked on her or his forehead. The baby is then taken out into the sunlight for a few minutes (care is taken that the baby does not get burnt by the sun). Offerings of new cloth, flowers and a coconut are taken to the mandir to give to the gods.

First foods

At about seven or eight months old, another samskara takes place. This is when the baby is given its first solid food. The child is fed rice, yoghurt, honey and ghee by his or her father.

Hair shaving

At some time after the first birthday, some children have their hair shaved off. Some Hindus believe that this removes bad karma, and some think that it makes the hair grow thick and strong. The barber is paid with money and food.

Ear piercing

In some Hindu traditions, children have their ears pierced when they reach the age of six. In other traditions, they have their ears pierced as part of the name-giving ceremony.

Why do you think the father feeds his child its first solid foods?

Look back

Karma (page 7)
Krishna (page 13)
Mandir (page 9)
Puja (page 27)
Samskara (page 48)

- At what age do Hindus sometimes have their ears pierced?
- Why do Hindu children have their heads shaved?
- What is the first solid food for a Hindu child?

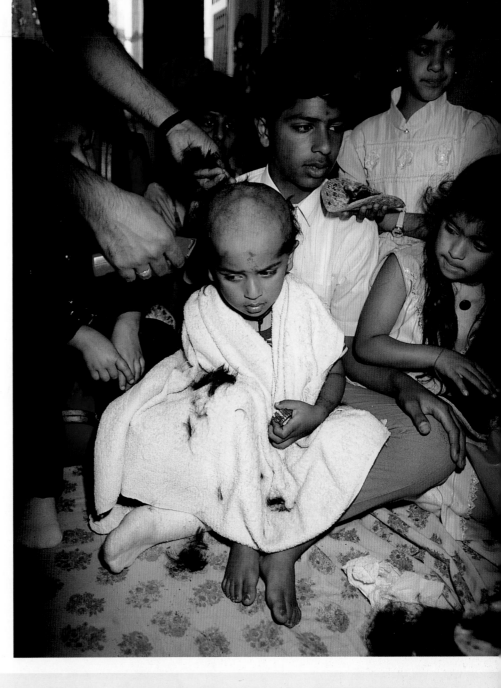

Describe what is happening in this picture.

1 a Does your name affect the way you behave or are treated by others?
b If you could have a different name, what would you choose? Explain why.

2 Imagine that you are invited to a baby-naming ceremony. Describe what happens in your own words.

3 Copy and complete a large version of the table on the right to explain the samskaras mentioned here. Add a drawing and a short description for each ritual.

Samskara	Drawing	What happens?

What happens when a Hindu grows up?

The wearing of the sacred thread is not only a samskara but it also marks the boy's entry into the first of the four ashramas. The ceremony means that it is the responsibility of male members of the household instead of his mother to guide and care for the boy,

Not all boys will wear a sacred thread: traditionally it has been the twice-born children who have had this honour. In Britain there is not so much attention to the caste laws, so many Hindus perform this ceremony to mark the time when the child becomes a young adult.

The wearing of the sacred thread reminds the boy that he has three main duties:

• Duty to God;

• Duty to his parents;

• Duty to the **gurus**, who will guide him through life.

During the sacred thread ceremony, the loop is placed over the boy's head so that it rests on his left shoulder and hangs down to his right hip. Apart from changing it once a year, it is worn for the rest of his life. Traditionally, the material the thread is made from varies according to the boy's status:

'The initiatory [first] thread of a brahmin should be made of cotton... three-ply, of a ruler it should be made of hemp threads, and of a commoner it should be wool threads.' (Laws of Manu 2:44)

This is how one young British Hindu described his sacred thread ceremony:

Saturday June 8th

I got my sacred thread today. I got up and washed and put on a new cotton shirt and my best trousers. The whole family did a special puja in front of our shrine in the front room. My uncle and cousins arrived at about 11 a.m. At about midday the priest arrived. I was told that in India I would have had my hair shaved off. As soon as the priest came, we all sat in the front room and a havan was lit. The priest read some prayers in sanskrit and prepared the thread. It is white and made from three strands. Dad said the Gayatri Mantra slowly and I repeated the words. I took my shirt off and put the thread on. The priest read another prayer and I got showered with rice whilst everyone sang.

At the end of the ceremony, the priest told me how important learning was and how I should respect my parents. Then I put my shirt back on. My uncle came up to me and chatted and then he gave me £20.

It is difficult to say how I felt after the ceremony. I did not feel much different but I did think my uncle treated me as a man instead of a boy. That was nice. I am going to buy a Walkman with the money.

- What is the sacred thread ceremony?
- Why is it important?
- How is the sacred thread worn?

For your dictionary

A **guru** is a holy man or teacher.

 Look back

Ashrama (page 48)
Brahmin (page 7)
Caste (page 7)
Gayatri Mantra (page 41)
Havan (page 37)
Puja (page 27)
Sacred thread (page 39)
Samskara (page 48)
Sanskrit (page 37)
Twice-born (page 7)

1 **a**   At what age do you think people grow out of childhood and start to take on their own responsibilities?
b   What decisions can adults make that children cannot?

2   Copy and complete the paragraph below:

The sacred thread ceremony is one of the Hindu s_____. A Hindu boy is given the thread to show that he has grown from c_____ into manhood. A priest comes into the boy's h_____ and performs the ceremony. The thread goes over the l_____ shoulder and under his right arm. The sacred thread has t_____ strands. These are a reminder of the boy's duty to God, to his parents and to his teacher. The thread is be worn next to the skin and changed once a year.

3   Re-read the diary extract.
a   What do you think the boy will remember most about the day?
b   Write down three clues from the diary which show us how important the family is to the boy.

4   The sacred thread reminds Hindu boys to do three duties. Below is the start of a poem which shows what these duties are. Finish the three verses, one for each duty.

'On this special day when I take the sacred thread,
I will spend my life honouring the words that I have said
To God and parents, to my teacher as well
I will look for truth
On good my mind will dwell
I will serve my God as best as I can by...
I will honour my parents by...
I will learn from my teacher by...

What happens when a Hindu gets married?

On these pages we shall look at Hindu marriage customs. On pages 74 and 75 we shall look at how brides and grooms meet each other. It is expected that Hindus will marry and have children. It is important to remember, however, that Hindu weddings take many different forms and may vary by caste, family, where you live, and so on.

Before the wedding

In India, most marriages take place between December and July to avoid the rainy season. A horoscope may be consulted to find out which day would be the best. Traditionally, the wedding would take place in the bride's home, but more often these days a hall is hired or the mandir community room is used. A few days before the wedding a special puja is said to Ganesha.

Preparations

In the past, wedding celebrations could go on for many days but nowadays they usually last for just one day. The bridegroom and all his family travel from their village to the hall where the wedding will take place. In the hall there is a shrine to Ganesha and to the gods of both families. A small stage with a canopy on top may be built in the middle of the room, and a havan is placed at the front of it. The guests sit all around the stage.

Hindu brides are prepared carefully: complicated patterns are painted onto the soles of her feet; her eyes are made up with a mixture of ghee, herbs and black make-up; and a red sari is worn.

The wedding service

- When the bridegroom arrives, he is offered a diva lamp and sweets or honey, and led to sit next to the bride.

- A simple puja is performed before the bride is given to the groom by placing her hand in his.

- They make promises to each other and walk seven steps around the havan.

- The couple then sit down and a piece of cotton thread is tied around each of their wrists. This symbolises that they are now bound together for life.

- The groom ties a necklace around the bride's neck and he takes her hand saying, 'I hope that we will grow old together.'

- The couple sit in front of the havan, the priest recites mantras and the husband and wife add wood, ghee, leaves, grain and water into the fire.

- To conclude the ceremony, they receive blessings and give each other garlands of flowers. The rest of the day is celebrated with food, dancing, music and everyone enjoying themselves.

How many steps will this couple take around the havan?

Some Hindus perform an extra ceremony, when the bride actually goes to live with her husband's family. It is often a time of great sadness, because she leaves her own family and becomes a part of his.

The seven steps

As we have read, the couple take seven steps around the havan. They hope for:

1   Food throughout their lives.

2   Strength and good health.

3   Wealth.

4   Happiness.

5   Children.

6   Enjoyment of the seasons.

7   Friendship for the rest of their lives.

- Where may a wedding take plece?
- What is poured into the havan?
- What is tied around the couple's wrists and what does it mean?

Why does the groom take the bride's hand?

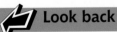 **Look back**

Caste (page 7)
Diva lamp (page 27)
Ganesha (page 23)
Ghee (page 9)
Havan (page 37)
Mandir (page 9)
Mantra (page 31)
Puja (page 27)

1 The bride and groom make promises to each other during the marriage. Write down five promises that you think are suitable for a couple to make when they get married.

2 a Write out the seven steps in the form of a poster that Hindus could put up at home to remind them of their wedding day.
b Which of the seven steps do you think are the most important to make a happy marriage?
c If you had to add one extra step, what would it be for? Explain why.

What happens when a Hindu dies?

The last samskara is cremation. In a religion where everything material passes away, it is easy to see why Hindus are cremated: the body is burnt but the **atman** can move on. There is no period of mourning, but death makes the relatives impure so Hindus have to become spiritually 'pure' again before they can return to normal life.

A funeral in India

When someone dies, they are dressed in new clothes and flowers are placed around the body. As soon as possible the body is taken to a river, preferably the Ganges, and placed on a funeral pyre (a pile of wood and dried cowdung, on which the body is burned). The face of the dead person is not covered up so that it can be seen. Red and yellow powders are put on the forehead and more flowers and incense are placed around the body.

The eldest son lights the pyre and the priest chants from the Vedas and the Bhagavad Gita. Oil is poured into the fire, and water is sprinkled on the ground around it. The pyre may burn for about an hour or so, and the ashes are collected and sprinkled into a river – ideally the River Ganges, as this is a very holy place where rivers meet. If this happens, Hindus believe the soul need not enter another body but will find peace.

Cremation in Britain

This is how one Hindu described his father's cremation:

'The body of my father was taken from the hospital to the funeral parlour and placed in a coffin. The family visited the parlour and I, being the eldest son, sprinkled from a container a little water from the River Ganges. We had collected the water when we went to Varanasi ten years ago. Flower garlands were placed around his neck. We all said our farewells and everyone was crying.

On the day of the cremation, the funeral car took the coffin straight to the crematorium. We arrived and followed the coffin in. The priest was there and he chanted 'Shanti'. I read from the Bhagavad Gita. After a short service, I had the honour of pressing the button which closed the curtains around the coffin. After the cremation, we were given the ashes so that we could scatter them out at sea.'

- Why do Hindus wish to scatter ashes of loved ones into the River Ganges?
- What responsibilities does the eldest son have?
- After a funeral, what do the family have to do before they can return to a normal life?

Why are Hindus cremated?

Look back

Bhagavad Gita (page 17)
Samskara (page 48)
Vedas (page 15)

For your dictionary

The **atman** is the indestructable part of us all – the soul. Hindus believe that the atman is part of God inside us all, which moves on to another body after death.

Where are the ashes usually sprinkled?

1 Read these extracts from the Bhagavad Gita:

'This soul residing [living] in the bodies of all can never be slain [destroyed]; therefore it does not behove you [it is not right] to grieve for anybody.' (Bhagavad Gita 2:30)

'The death of him who is born is certain; and the rebirth of him who is dead is inevitable.' (Bhagavad Gita 2:27)

a Explain in your own words what each extract is saying.
b What do these extracts teach us about what Hindus think happens to the soul after death?

2 Copy and complete a large version of the following table by writing each of the following statements in the correct column. Some of the statements may go in both columns.

Cremation in India	Cremation in Britain

a The body is taken to the funeral parlour and placed in a coffin.
b The body is taken to the nearby river.
c A pyre is built using wood and slabs of dried cowdung.
d The face of the dead person is left uncovered and coloured powders are placed on the forehead.
e Water from the River Ganges is sprinkled over the body.
f Flowers are placed around the body.
g The eldest son lights the pyre.
h The eldest son presses the button so that the curtains are closed.
i The ashes are collected and sprinkled in the river or in the sea.

3 Why are there differences between Indian and British cremations? Choose two examples and explain why you think things are done differently.

Why do Hindus go on pilgrimage?

Hindus go on **pilgrimage** for many different reasons. Some Hindus think that they should go on pilgrimage at least once in their lifetime, others many times, while others believe it is optional. India is well known for its many holy places, and millions of Hindus from India and throughout the world visit these places.

For some Hindus the journey may be long and tiring, often spending many hours on crowded trains and buses or travelling by foot. However, Hindus believe that the greater the effort in making the pilgrimage, the more good karma they will get from it. Some Hindus even walk barefoot in the snows of the Himalayas and bathe in the icy source of the River Ganges.

Pilgrimage sites

Many places have become special over the years:

*   Rivers. There are seven sacred rivers in India, of which the River Ganges is the most holy. Some people believe that bathing in the water will remove all bad karma. To have your ashes sprinkled into the water ensures freedom from **samsara**. The source of rivers or places where two or more rivers meet are considered very holy.

*   The Himalayas. It was once thought that the gods lived in the Himalayas: Shiva's home, Kailasa, is in the mountains, and to struggle up to his shrine brings great rewards.

*   Mandirs. There are many stories of great things happening at the numerous shrines and mandirs. Hindus are attracted to places linked to their own particular god or goddess, and to pay them a visit brings spiritual benefit.

*   Towns. Certain towns are considered sacred, for example, Varanasi, which is special because it is on the banks of the River Ganges.

Make a list of the pilgrimage sites shown on this map.

Why go on pilgrimage?

Some Hindus go on pilgrimage to pray quietly to their gods, others go to large religious fairs and festivals and join in with massive crowds. There are huge bathing fairs at Hardwar on the River Ganges every 12 years. Million of Hindus go there to try to bathe in the river. Special nets are lowered from the bridges so that people do not get washed down the river.

Another reason why Hindus go on pilgrimage is because they have asked their God for a special favour. If the favour is granted, they visit that God's shrine to give thanks.

Pilgrimages are also made to sprinkle the ashes of a dead relative in a holy place, or because the pilgrim has sinned or done something bad and they hope to wipe away any bad karma.

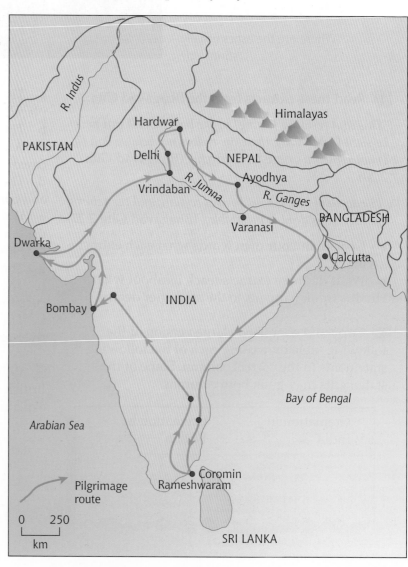

Hindus at Varanasi, on the banks of the River Ganges. Why do many Hindus go there?

For your dictionary

A **pilgrimage** is a special journey to a holy place.
Samsara is the cycle of birth, life, death and reincarnation in which everyone is caught up.

- What is a pilgrimage?
- Why do Hindus go to Hardwar?
- Where is Varanasi?

 Look back

Karma (page 7)
Mandir (page 9)
Reincarnation (page 5)
Shiva (page 7)

1 What is the difference between a tourist and a pilgrim?

2 Imagine you are planning to go on a pilgrimage.
a   What would you do to prepare for the journey?
b   What would you pack, and why?
c   What would you do to make the journey less comfortable?
d   What would you hope to gain from your journey?

3 Design a brochure from a travel agency advertising a tour of pilgrimage sites in India. You could mention:
a   travel arrangements.
b   a description of the hotels.
c   what pilgrims can do when they arrive at each site.
d   any background information or interesting stories about the sites.
e   what makes your travel company special.

You may wish to cut out pictures from old travel brochures to make your brochure more interesting.

Holy people
Who is Sathya Sai Baba?

A great many people have influenced Hinduism. Over the next few pages we will look at some of these people and their ideas. These examples have been chosen to show how different people have made changes to Hinduism, but it is important to remember that not all Hindus believe that the people mentioned here are important or even right.

Early life

Sathya Sai Baba was born in a small village in southern India on 23 November 1926. Some people say that **miracles** happened when he was born: a snake crawled into the crib to protect the baby and musical instruments played by themselves. As a child he became known for his kindness, generosity and wisdom. The name Sai Baba means Divine Father.

In 1940, when he was 14 years old, he told his family and friends that he wanted to spend the rest of his life teaching people that the most important things are truth, right behaviour, peace, love and non-violence.

The three avatars

Sathya Sai Baba is believed to be the second time the Sai avatar has come to the earth. The first Sai avatar was Shirdi Sai Baba, a holy man who died in 1918. The third and final incarnation will come after the present Sai Baba has died, and will be known as Prema Sai Baba.

His work

Sathya Sai Baba is a highly respected teacher and spiritual leader. Each year, thousands of people from many different faiths go on pilgrimage to his **ashram**, where for more than 50 years he has walked among the people to give them guidance, comfort and support.

When did Sathya Sai Baba begin his mission to 'Love All, Serve All'?

He considers proper education for young people to be of the utmost importance, so he has set up many schools and universities which anybody can attend, no matter how much money they have or what religion they belong to.

His message and teachings

Sathya Sai Baba believes that if people follow their conscience then their thoughts, words and actions will be worthy and pure. In trusting our conscience, we will recognise that we are all united in the one God.

He urges people to help the sick and the needy, to respect the laws of the country in which they live, to faithfully follow their own religions, and to respect all other religions:

'Let the different faiths exist, let them flourish [thrive], and let the glory of God be sung in all the languages and a variety of tunes.'

- Which Sai avatar is Sathya Sai Baba?
- How old was he when he declared his mission?
- What does he believe humankind should follow?

For your dictionary

An **ashram** is a place for spiritual development.
A **miracle** is an event which seems to be outside the usual laws of nature.

Look back

Avatar (page 13)
Pilgrimage (page 59)

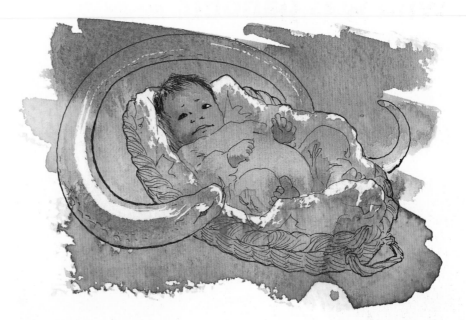

What miracles happened when Sathya Sai Baba was born?

 Read this quotation by someone who has visited Sathya Sai Baba:

'Sathya Sai Baba is an amazing man. He does not mind who comes to him – Muslim, Christian, Hindu, everyone. We went to India to visit him in his ashram. Even though there were thousands of people there, it felt like he was talking directly to me. My friend was ill so she hoped that Sai Baba could heal her. As she sat listening to him, she was healed. He did not have to touch her or even talk to her. His spirit is so strong that he can heal, just like that.'

Describe in your own words what this person is saying.

2 Do you think that miracles can happen? Copy this table into your book and list your arguments.

Arguments for	Arguments against

3 When talking about the many different world religions, Sathya Sai Baba has said that it is not necessary to drink the whole ocean to know its taste. What do you think he means?

4 Imagine being in a crowd of thousands listening to Sathya Sai Baba. Write a short newspaper report about all you see and hear. Remember that you should write with respect, whatever you believe.

Who was Gandhi?

Mohandas Gandhi is possibly the most admired Hindu in the world. He became well known for his non-violent protest against prejudice in South Africa and against British rule in India. He became known as 'Mahatma' (meaning 'great soul'), and was often called Gandhiji – adding the letters 'ji' to a name is a mark of respect, showing that the person is very special.

Can you suggest why Gandhi chose to dress in this way?

Early years

The son of a government minister, he was born in 1869 in western India and trained in Britain to become a lawyer. At the age of 24, he moved to South Africa, where he worked very hard to try to improve the rights of Indians living there. During this time he stressed the importance of **ahimsa** and **satyagraha.** He was sure that the only way to solve all problems was through non-violence.

Struggles in India

In 1915 he moved back to India with his wife and family. He believed that his country should not be ruled by Britain, so he urged people to refuse to buy clothes made in Britain and to spin their own cloth. Everywhere he went he taught people to use a spinning wheel, which became a symbol of independence.

Gandhi would often fast to try to change people's points of view. When Muslims and Hindus fought, whether against each other or against the British, he fasted until the fighting stopped.

Tolerance

Gandhi was a strong believer in religious tolerance – although he was Hindu himself, he thought people should be allowed to practise whatever religion they choose. He was against the caste system because it caused so much hardship amongst the poor. He renamed the untouchables 'harijans', which means 'children of God':

'I would far rather that Hinduism died than untouchability lived.'

Gandhi's death

On 30 January 1948, at the age of 79, he was shot and killed as he was on his way to take evening prayers in New Delhi.

 **Look back**

Caste (page 7)
Fast (page 33)

For your dictionary

Ahimsa means non-violence.
Satyagraha means 'truth force'. Gandhi's search for Truth (i.e. God) was his lifelong goal, and he believed that non-violence was the way to reach this goal.

- By what other names was Mohandas Gandhi known?
- What is ahimsa?
- What symbol came to represent independence for India?

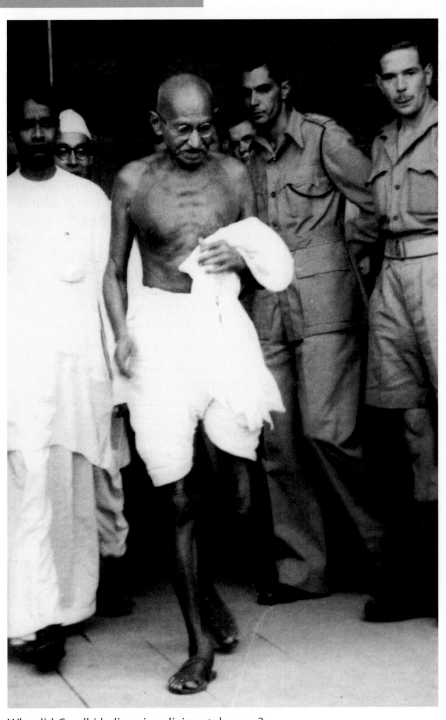

Why did Gandhi believe in religious tolerance?

1 Read this quotation:

'The world cannot subsist [exist] for a single moment without yajna. Yajna means an act directed to the welfare of others, done without desiring any return for it, whether of a temporal [material] or spiritual nature. "Act" here must be taken in its widest sense, and includes thought and word as well as deed.' (Gandhi)

a Use Gandhi's words to create a poster to show the meaning of yajna.
b Give two examples of times when you have acted with yajna.

2 Read the following quotations by Gandhi and explain, in your own words, what he was saying:

- 'Non-violence is the greatest force at the disposal of mankind. It is mightier than the mightiest weapon of destruction devised by the ingenuity of man.'

- 'Even as a tree has a single trunk but many branches and leaves, there is one religion – human religion – but any number of faiths.'

- 'My religion teaches me that whenever there is distress which one cannot remove, one must fast and pray.'

- 'Ahimsa and Truth are my two lungs.'

63

Who are the other swamis and gurus?

ISKCON stands for the International Society for Krishna Consciousness. It arrived in Britain in 1968 and was soon a success, gaining a song in the charts which reached number 12. Many musicians were drawn to the group after George Harrison of The Beatles helped the Krishna mandir devotees to produce a number of records. It was not their aim to become great pop stars but to let all the people of Britain know about Krishna Consciousness.

Their guru was A C Bhaktivedanta Swami Prabhupada, who was born in 1896 in Calcutta, India. In 1953 he retired from family life to become a holy man. He studied the works of a sixteenth-century Hindu monk and told everyone that the way to moksha was through **bhakti-yoga**.

In 1965 he went to America, arriving with just his clothes and seven dollars. He soon found many followers amongst the people who lived there and he taught them about bhakti-yoga. Before his death in 1977, he had set up many ISKCON centres, written many books and spread the ISKCON movement in both Britain and America.

Lord Swaminarayan

Lord Swaminarayan was born in India in 1781. He had mastered the holy books by the age of ten, and by the age of 11 he had become a holy man. He had many followers and founded a community of 500 monks. He lived with the poorest of people and his community helped to educate them. He believed in non-violence and he formed a religious community of women with female preachers. He died at the age of 49 in 1830.

Since his death there have been five leaders of this community. The latest leader is Pramukh Swami Maharaj, who has inspired the beautiful mandir in Neasden, North London (see page 42).

Jalaram Bapa

Jalaram Bapa was a trader who lived in Gujurat at the beginning of the nineteenth century. He was reknowned for helping other people – it is believed that Rama visited him, disguised as an old man, and Jalaram took him in and fed him.

Hindus are reminded to follow Jalaram's example and treat well everyone they meet, because the stranger could be God visiting them in disguise.

Who was the founder of Krishna Consciousness?

Members of ISKCON in London. Why do you think they dress like this?

Look back

Guru (page 53)
Krishna (page 13)
Mandir (page 9)
Moksha (page 5)
Rama (page 13)

For your dictionary

Bhakti-yoga is the path of loving devotion to God.
Hare means lord.
A **swami** is a religious teacher or holy person.

- What does ISKCON stand for?
- What has been built in memory of Lord Swaminarayan?
- Who was Jalaram Bapa?

1 ISKCON followers believe that by chanting the following words they can clear their minds of everything but God.

'**Hare** *Krishna, Hare Krishna, Krishna Krishna, Hare Hare, Hare Rama, Hare Rama, Rama Rama, Hare Hare.*'

How can chanting the words of Hare Krishna be seen as bhakti-yoga?

2 What do all the holy people on these pages have in common?

3 Who would you choose as a role model to inspire you to behave well?

What do Hindus think about animals?

Hindus recognise that animals have feelings and believe that their souls are reincarnated into different life forms over time. Animals are treated with respect because God has appeared on the earth in the form of animals and many of the gods have animals as their servants. Shiva has a servant who is Nandi the bull, and Krishna is often linked with the cow.

Vegetarianism

It is not true to say that all Hindus are and have always been **vegetarians**. Some Hindus eat meat, but most do not. Hindus teach that vegetarianism is a way of life which causes the least hurt to other beings.

Here are some reasons given by a Hindu about why she is a vegetarian:

- In the scriptures, we are taught about the importance of ahimsa, and that includes non-violence towards animals.

- Karma – all actions have consequences. If pain is caused to animals then we must experience the same pain in the future.

- Food affects us – we are what we eat. Meat causes bad feelings like anger, jealousy and fear.

- Vegetarians are healthier than meat eaters, with fewer medical problems.

- Environmental reasons – three times more fossil fuels are used in cooking meat than in cooking vegetables.

Food laws

In ancient times, Hindus sacrificed animals and ate meat:

'An animal sacrifice at the end of every half year.'
(Laws of Manu 4:26)

'He should put down on the ground before priests seasoned foods like soups and vegetables... tasty meats.'
(Laws of Manu 3:227)

What can you tell from this photograph about Hindu belief in animals?

Hindus are encouraged not to eat meat and should certainly not eat meat which 'is given disrespectfully or... meat without a sacrificial purpose.' (*Laws of Manu 3:213*)

The cow

To many Hindus, cows are important animals. They provide us with milk and butter, dung for fuel and building material, and they are useful for pulling ploughs or carts. These are not the only reasons cattle are treated with great respect – Hindus consider them to be sacred animals:

'The very name of cow is aghnya ["not to be killed"], indicating that they should never be slaughtered. Who, then, could slay [kill] them? Surely one who kills a cow or a bull commits a heinous [terrible] crime.'
(Mahabharata 262:47)

In Britain, ISKCON devotees (see pages 64 and 65) have established a model farm to show how the cow should be treated, and during the BSE crisis many Hindus were appalled at the idea of destroying so many animals.

How many different types of food do you recognise here?

- What is a vegetarian?
- Why is the cow sacred to Hindus?
- Who was Shiva's servant and what sort of animal was he?

For your dictionary

A **vegetarian** is someone who does not eat any meat or fish. The sanskrit word for a vegetarian is 'shakahari'.

Look back

1 Read these two quotations about food laws and explain in your own words what each one means:

'One who partakes of human flesh, the flesh of a horse or another animal, and deprives others of milk by slaughtering cows, O King, if such a fiend does not desist [stop] by other means, then you should not hesitate to cut off his head.' (Rig Veda 10.87.16)

'Anyone who looks carefully at the source of meat, and at the tying up and slaughter of animals should turn back from eating meat.' (Laws of Manu 5:49)

2 Divide a clean page into two columns. In the left column, write the heading 'Evidence for vegetarianism' and in the right column write 'Evidence against vegetarianism'. Write down as many points as you can for and against eating meat.

3 Write about 100 words to explain your own views on meat-eating.

How do Hindus view violence?

When the caste system was in place there was a varna called Kshatriyas – the warriors. It was their duty to rule, preserve order and fight if necessary. It was not a sin for these people to fight – it was their **dharma-yuddha**.

Holy war

The Bhagavad Gita describes a great battle and the God Krishna urges Arjuna, the hero of the story, to fight:

'For there is nothing more welcome for a man of the warrior caste than a righteous war.' (Bhagavad Gita 2:31)

Many Hindus do not take the story of the Bhagavad Gita literally – they believe that the 'war' is against sins such as addiction and greed. Other Hindus think the message is that they can fight in a war as long as it is 'righteous'.

Ahimsa

Hindus are often considered to be non-violent people. This is probably largely due to the fact that Gandhi achieved independence in India by ahimsa.

*'Ahimsa is the highest **dharma**. Ahimsa is the greatest gift. Ahimsa is the highest self-control. Ahimsa is the highest truth. Ahimsa is the highest.'* (Mahabharata 18:37–41)

Many Hindus have taken these words and tried to live by ahimsa. As one Hindu explained, 'we oppose killing for many reasons:

- We believe in karma and reincarnation. If we cause hurt, we will experience the same hurt in a later life.

- We should not have emotions of anger or jealousy because they distract us from our concentration on God.

- We believe that every person has a part of God inside them. If I use violence, I am hurting God.'

- What is dharma-yuddha?
- Which Hindu holy book describes a battle?
- What can Hindus 'fight' against today?

What is a 'righteous' war?

The cycle of violence

Sita: shouts at her secretary, Gopal, and tells him to retype a letter.

Gopal: retypes the letter but misses his bus home. When he gets home he shouts at his daughter, Lakshmi, for having an untidy room.

Lakshmi: tidies her room but is late for meeting her friend, Neela. She shouts at Neela because she feels guilty for being late.

Vijay: gets so angry with Neela that she is grounded; he then he shouts at his wife, Sita.

Neela: goes home unhappy and upsets her father, Vijay, by refusing to talk to him.

In real life, anger does not always get passed back to the person who started it. When we are faced with an angry person, we have several options:
* We can pass the anger back.
* We can pass the anger on.
* We can use ahimsa and stop the circle of violence.

Only one of these choices makes the world a better place – ahimsa.

> ### For your dictionary
> **Dharma** means moral duty.
> **Dharma-yuddha** is the duty for a warrior to fight in a righteous war.

⬅ Look back

Ahimsa (page 63)
Bhagavad Gita (page 17)
Caste (page 7)
Karma (page 7)
Krishna (page 13)
Mahabharata (page 87)
Reincarnation (page 5)
Varna (page 7)

1 Make up your own cycle of violence. How could the cycle be broken?

2 Write a paragraph to explain Hindu belief in dharma-yuddha.

3 a What does 'righteous' mean?
b Can you think of any wars which might be seen as 'righteous'? Write down as many as you can and explain why you chose these.

4 Give an example where non-violence has solved a problem.

What is satyagraha?

Satyagraha is not new to Hinduism, but Gandhi placed his own particular meaning upon the word. It is made up of two words: 'satya' meaning 'truth' and 'graha' meaning 'to seize or overpower'. A 'grah' was a demon who would overpower people and take possession of them. Gandhi believed that the Truth could seize a person and take possession of her or him.

Gandhi believed that everybody has a little of God's spirit inside them. This is called the atman. If that spirit could take possession of the person, it would change her or him from a bad person into a good person.

Methods of satyagraha

Gandhi spoke about 'creative suffering' as a way to bring about satyagraha. If a person is hitting you, take the punishment and do not fight back. That is satyagraha. Eventually the person might realise that hitting you is wrong. Unfortunately you might have to die to convince them. The aim is to use the force of truth to bring about changes in that person:

'Satyagraha can rid society of all evils – political, economic and moral.' (Gandhi)

Another method is to be prepared to fast until death. If everyone knows why you are fasting, and the cause is for the reason of truth, satyagraha will be able to work.

As Hindus believe in reincarnation, if they die as a result of satyagraha then they have achieved two things: the changing of the bad person and good karma for their own rebirth.

Satyagraha in action

When Gandhi was in South Africa, all Indians had to carry passes to allow them to travel. This was unfair as it meant that they could be stopped at any time and asked to show their passes. No white people had to carry passes.

Copy this illustration and explain what it is trying to show.

Gandhi led the resistance against this law by using satyagraha. When he and his fellow Indians burnt their passes, they were beaten – but they did not fight back. They were put in prison but still many Indians refused to carry passes. The prisons became so full that in the end the government had to change the law. The force of Truth had won a battle without anyone fighting the 'enemy'.

What is happening in this picture? Explain how this could be an act of satyagraha.

- What does satyagraha mean?
- What takes over in satyagraha?
- How did Gandhi use satyagraha?

Look back

Atman (page 57)
Fast (page 33)
Karma (page 7)
Reincarnation (page 5)
Satyagraha (page 63)

1 Copy and complete the following sentences:
a   The word satyagraha comes from two words: satya and _____.

b   Hindus believe that everyone has a part of God inside them and this is called the _____.
c   The way that satyagraha works is that the victim has to be prepared to _____ or even _____.
d   The aim is to convince others using the force of _____.

2 Write out a short story to show how a school bully was changed by satyagraha.

3 Do you think that satyagraha is only possible if you are a Hindu who believes in reincarnation and karma?

How are Hindu women viewed?

If you ask some people in Britain about Hindu women, they will tell you about inequalities and poorly treated women. But it is not wise to judge Indian society on the same terms as British. Hindu women in the past may have had to obey their husbands without question, but we should remember that Indian women had power in the family.

In modern times, Hindu women go to clubs and dance, they are important businesswomen, they have careers as doctors and architects, models and filmstars, and one woman, Indira Gandhi (who was not related to Mahatma Gandhi), has been India's Prime Minister.

Dress

The traditional dress is the sari. It covers the body, legs and arms against the fierce Indian sun, whilst keeping the wearer as cool as possible. A sari is about five or six metres of cloth, sometimes worn so that the stomach is bare. Some of the material of the sari can be pulled over the head. Hindu women from the Punjab may wear a shalwar kameez instead of the sari. The kameez is a long shirt and the shalwar are loose trousers. But traditional dress has not always been the same: there are fashions in colour, fabric, style and embroidery. Many young Hindus wear western clothes all or most of the time.

Jewellery

Many Hindu women wear jewellery. Some of the jewellery is just fashion, but some pieces are very important. Much of this jewellery is so special that it is never removed. A woman might wear:

- ears and nose pierced with studs or rings.

- the many glass and gold bangles she received when she got married.

- several wedding necklaces containing precious stones.

- medallions with pictures of their gurus on them.

- special protective bangles which they believe will protect them from illness.

After having a child, a Hindu woman may wear a gold bangle given to her by her sister-in-law in the seventh month of pregnancy.

The bindi or tilak

Many Hindu women wear a small bindi spot on their foreheads. Traditionally this would show that a woman is married but nowadays some unmarried women choose to wear them as a fashion accessory. The colour usually matches their clothes. If they have just performed puja, they might have a tilak spot placed on their forehead by the priest.

What position did Indira Gandhi hold in India?

What are these women's dresses called?

- What is a shalwar kameez?
- What is a bindi?
- What is a tilak?

 Look back

Guru (page 53)
Puja (page 27)

1 Design a pattern for a modern sari. You could include some Hindu symbols on it.

2 Find out more about Indira Gandhi and write a short biography of her life.

3 In this crossword you have the answers but the clues are missing. Make up your own short clues to go with each answer.

What do Hindus think about marriage?

Hindus often do not choose their own marriage partners. Even though there are more love marriages taking place, many Hindus will have an arranged, or 'assisted', marriage. In Britain, marriage is the union of a man and a woman; in India it is the joining of two groups of people. People in India believe marriage is for a different purpose, and have different expectations than in Britain.

Finding a partner

When a woman is old enough to get married, word passes through a close-knit network of relatives, friends and associates that she is looking for a husband. Her parents consult a priest and a horoscope is drawn up. The parents and relations try to find someone to suit her personality.

When several possible partners have been found, she is visited, in the company of female relatives, by each one in turn. If they like each other, their parents will discuss the plans for the wedding and the future of the couple.

In Britain today many Hindus fall in love and find their own partners. These are called love marriages. It is an interesting fact that more love marriages fail than assisted marriages – perhaps the choosing of a partner is more difficult than we think!

Divorce

Most people would like to think that when they get married it is for life. Of course, this does not always happen. Divorce in India has been legal since 1955, but it is not common. The break-up of a marriage is deeply felt by everyone concerned: it affects the couple, their families, the community and the Hindu faith. After divorce, the woman might have to live on her own without help from anyone and she might not be able to get work.

This woman is being prepared for marriage. What expectations might she have of her future life?

What might this couple believe about marriage?

- What is an assisted marriage?
- What is a love marriage?
- How do many Hindus find marriage partners?

Look back

Caste (page 7)

1 Read this quotation by a man who was happy to have an assisted marriage:

'When I graduated from university, I worked for a year. Then I took a month's holiday and went back to India. Whilst I was there, my family arranged for me to meet several young ladies. I found one I liked and we got married. I travelled back to Britain alone and she joined me a few weeks later. We are very happy. We have grown to love each other.'

a What are the good things about assisted marriages?
b In what ways might family members be better at choosing suitable marriage partners?

2 Read this quotation by a Hindu living in Britain:

'When I was in India, I thought that I would marry my children to the correct caste and style. Here in Britain I have had to lower my expectations. I would be delighted if my son married someone with Indian origins – even if she is of a different religion.'

a How does this show that customs are changing in Britain?
b What problems might occur if his son married someone from a different religion?

3 Many people in Britain are against assisted marriages. However, some people are now using computer dating to find the perfect partner. What is the difference between the two?

4 Write a short article called 'Hindus and assisted marriages' for a newspaper. Consider all the reasons for and against assisted marriage and then sum up by adding your own views.

What do Hindus believe about reincarnation and karma?

Many people believe that when you die there must be 'something else'. Hindus believe that when you die you are reincarnated, or reborn. All living things have an atman inside them. When a plant or animal dies, the atman must be reborn higher up the ladder of reincarnation. Humans are different: the way you have lived your life affects whether your atman is reborn higher up or lower down the ladder.

Karma

Some Hindus talk about **merit** and sins. Good karma gains merit and allows a Hindu to be reincarnated higher up the ladder. Bad karma or sins do the opposite. Every action a human makes, or even *thinks*, carries karma. Even a good action which is done for the wrong reason can attract bad karma.

'*As a man takes off worn-out clothes, and puts on new ones, likewise the atman casts off worn-out bodies, enters into others which are new.*' (Bhagavad Gita 2:22)

When a human dies there is no judge or weighing machine. Certain bad karma automatically ensures that you will be reborn in certain forms. Only the special rites of death and the sprinkling of ashes in the River Ganges may alter this (see pages 56 and 57).

What is this drawing trying to explain?

What is the ultimate goal of all Hindus?

Look back

Atman (page 57)
Bhagavad Gita (page 17)
Karma (page 7)
Moksha (page 5)
Reincarnation (page 5)

For your dictionary

Merit is the spiritual reward that comes from doing good deeds.

- What is the atman?
- Where are atmans found?
- What is the lowest level of reincarnation?

1 Read this quotation about reincarnation by a young Hindu:

'When you were a baby you had one body. It looked very different to the body you have now. All the cells in that old body have died and you have all new cells. There is nothing in your new body that was in your old body – except your atman! When you get older you will have another body, different to the one that you have now. The atman has passed from one body to another to another. It is not so strange to think that when you die, the atman will go into another new body. That is reincarnation.'

a Draw a picture to illustrate this extract.
b Why is the atman important?

2 There is a Hindu game much like 'snakes and ladders'. To climb a ladder the square tells you that you have done something to gain good karma (for example, helping your grandmother). Squares where snakes start are for bad karma (for example, lying to your parents).

Draw a snakes and ladders game using karma as your reasons for going up ladders and down snakes. Remember, you must do something pretty bad to go down a long snake! The first person to escape rebirth and enter moksha is the winner. The game is played until everyone reaches moksha – and then it starts all over again. That is just like the Hindu belief in reincarnation.

What do Hindus think about moksha?

> Moksha is the final stage of existence, when the atman is freed from the long cycle of birth, death and rebirth. Hindus believe that all atmans will eventually be freed to be joined with the Supreme Spirit, Brahman.

Moksha is sometimes called 'heaven', but this is not quite right. Some Hindus believe in heaven and hell but they are only temporary places to wait until the atman is reborn again. There are four main ways to reach moksha – bhakti-yoga, **jnana-yoga**, **karma-yoga** and **raja-yoga** – and many Hindus follow more than one path.

Bhakti-yoga

This means personal devotion – chanting prayers and offering love and devotion – to a deity. ISKCON members follow this path towards moksha (see pages 64 and 65).

Jnana-yoga

This yoga means 'the path of knowledge'. This does not mean that Hindus have to learn the Vedas and then be tested on them. The knowledge is not facts themselves but the ability to be able to tell what will lead you to moksha and what is **maya**.

For example, think about the choice between doing your homework or going to the cinema. Homework could lead to passing exams; going to the cinema could lead to failing exams. The pleasure of going to the cinema would be maya because it would not last long and is a distraction from studying. However, it *could* be that the film is important for your studies, so then it would not be maya. The ability to tell what leads to maya and what leads to moksha is the path of jnana-yoga.

Karma-yoga

This is simply that all actions you make have consequences; if not in this life then in your future lives. Hindus believe that every good deed must be done without expecting a reward in return. Your duty (dharma) may differ depending on which caste you belong to. For example, touching a dead body might bring bad karma to one Hindu, but good karma to another.

Raja-yoga

Raja literally means 'kingly'. Raja-yoga is the path of meditation. Some Hindus will perfect their ability to meditate and so they believe that when they die their atman will leave the body and achieve moksha.

Which yoga is this man following?

- Which path is followed by meditation?
- What is the aim of all the yogas?
- Which path guides you into performing selfless deeds?

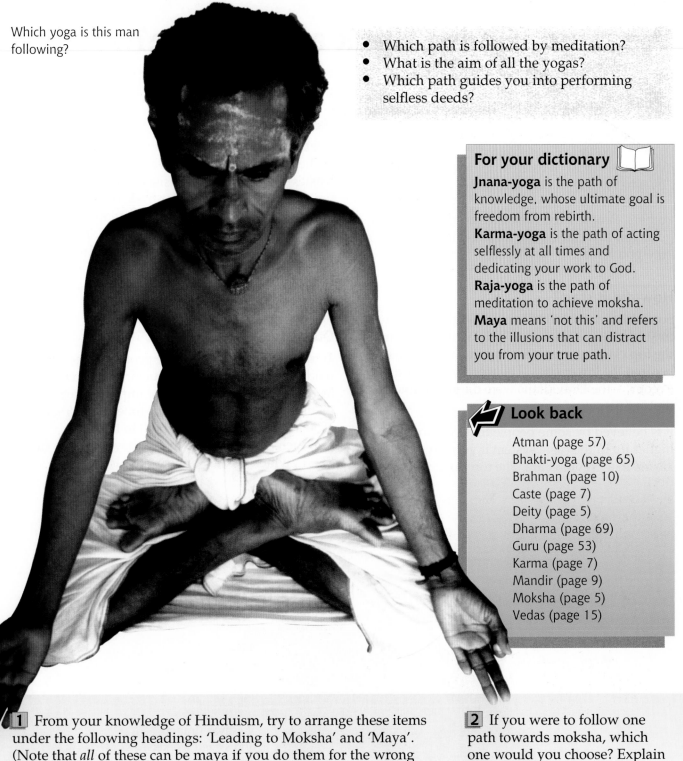

For your dictionary 📖

Jnana-yoga is the path of knowledge, whose ultimate goal is freedom from rebirth.
Karma-yoga is the path of acting selflessly at all times and dedicating your work to God.
Raja-yoga is the path of meditation to achieve moksha.
Maya means 'not this' and refers to the illusions that can distract you from your true path.

Look back

Atman (page 57)
Bhakti-yoga (page 65)
Brahman (page 10)
Caste (page 7)
Deity (page 5)
Dharma (page 69)
Guru (page 53)
Karma (page 7)
Mandir (page 9)
Moksha (page 5)
Vedas (page 15)

1 From your knowledge of Hinduism, try to arrange these items under the following headings: 'Leading to Moksha' and 'Maya'. (Note that *all* of these can be maya if you do them for the wrong reason!)

Doing homework   Going to cinema   Drinking alcohol

Visiting grandmother   Going to mandir   Eating meat

Getting married   Hitting someone   Visiting your guru

2 If you were to follow one path towards moksha, which one would you choose? Explain why.

3 What is your main goal in life? Write down which of your actions lead you towards your main goal.

What do Hindus think about caste?

In Britain today, many people believe that everyone is, or should be, equal. Ancient Indians did not hold that belief. They thought that equality was impossible and society was meant to be unequal but fair. The system was based on impurity – most of us are impure to some extent by what we do, touch, or eat, but the jobs people do make them purer or less pure than others. People lived their lives according to their position and carried out their separate duties for the good of all.

How did it start?

Some historians will tell you that when India was invaded (see pages 6 and 7), the winners became the top classes (or varnas) and the Dravidians became the lower class. The word varna means 'colour' – the Dravidians were darker skinned than the Aryans.

It is believed by some people that you are born higher up in the caste system if you have had good karma in a previous life. The top three varnas are often called twice-born as they have already lived good lives as a shudra.

Varna and jati

There are four main varnas (see diagram) and each of these is subdivided into thousands of jatis (castes). A jati usually consists of about a thousand families who have a similar trade or profession. For example, the potter jati is made up of about a thousand families who are all potters. They pass the skills of their trade on to their children. They expect their children to marry others from the same jati. The word caste is wrongly used by many people to describe both varna and jati!

Outcastes

Traditionally, these were the people whose jobs made them impure. Even touching them could lead a caste person to become impure. They included leather workers and toilet cleaners. In 1950 a law was passed in India to make 'untouchability' illegal. Today they like to be called 'dalit', which means 'of no caste'.

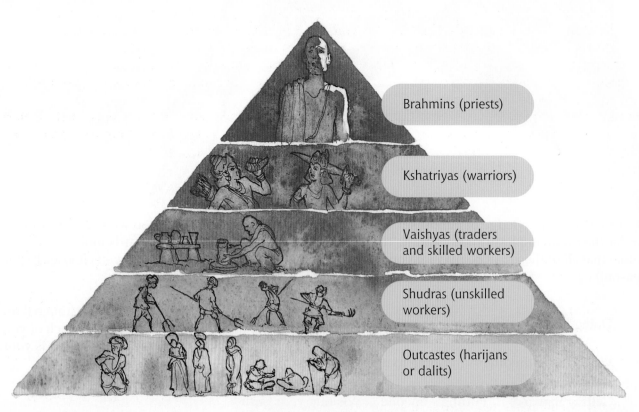

Brahmins (priests)

Kshatriyas (warriors)

Vaishyas (traders and skilled workers)

Shudras (unskilled workers)

Outcastes (harijans or dalits)

What is a varna?

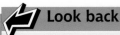

Look back

Aryans (page 7)
Brahmin (page 7)
Caste (page 7)
Dravidians (page 7)
Karma (page 7)
Mandir (page 9)
Twice-born (page 7)
Varna (page 7)

- What is the Hindu name for the warrior varna?
- Roughly how many families are there in a jati?
- Why is caste less important today than it used to be?

Traditionally, which caste would these people have belonged to?

The old rules

In India in ancient times, few people travelled very far. Therefore, the villages had to be self-sufficient. It made sense for each village to have one potter, one carpenter, and so on. When it was time to get married, a person from the same trade – but a different village – would be found. The trade continued, everyone had a place in life and a job to do. They each provided services for the others, so they depended on each other. Members of the same caste ate with each other, not with people from different castes.

Changes

Changes are being made for one simple reason: money. Traditionally, no one was paid money. The caste system relied on everyone doing their job and so everyone was fed. Today, people are paid money for their work and they travel together on the same bus to the same factory (they cannot have different buses from the same village).

In Britain, Hindus from all castes worship in the same mandir. There is still prejudice but it is gradually declining. A low caste child in Britain can go to university alongside a high caste child.

1 Copy and complete these sentences:
a Caste was useful in villages because...
b The word 'varna' means...
c The word 'jati' means...
d Historians think the caste system started when...
e Leather workers, butchers and toilet cleaners were outcastes because in Hinduism these jobs were thought to be...

2 In Britain we do not have a caste system but we do have something a little similar.
a List these jobs in order of importance:

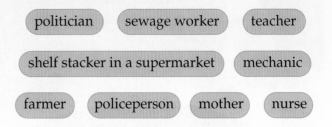

politician   sewage worker   teacher

shelf stacker in a supermarket   mechanic

farmer   policeperson   mother   nurse

b Explain why you have chosen this order.

What do Hindus think about sex, drugs, abortion and genetic engineering?

It is wrong to say that all Hindus think in the same way. People are born into a Hindu family and society and this defines how they behave. There is enormous freedom of thought. There is as much difference of opinion between young and old Hindus as there is between young and old of any religion. In this section we shall look at a few Hindu beliefs. But remember that we are all different and as such we are entitled to our own views.

Sex

Hindu literature celebrates the act of sex. The *Karma Sutra* is an Indian holy book. As sex is part of everyday life, Hindus believe that it is part of their dharma. Generally, it is believed that sex is best within marriage. Although some people may not wait until after marriage, this is disapproved of by the community.

The story of the Ramayana is often used to show how Sita remained faithful to Rama, even after she had been kidnapped (see pages 18–19 and 92–93).

Contraception

Most Hindu couples have no religious reasons for not using contraception. In India there have been government campaigns designed to get couples to have less children to improve maternal and child health, and to reduce population growth.

It is traditional for Hindus to want to have children, and to keep on having them until they have at least one son. Some Hindu women are very modest and so will not use contraception if it means visiting a male doctor. Some poor people in India might not be able to afford contraception so they may choose to have an operation to stop them having children.

How is the story of Sita and Rama used as an example to others?

Abortion

Traditionally, Hindus are against abortion as it can be seen as an act which would attract bad karma. The atman of the aborted foetus would be reincarnated but the mother might gain bad karma. However, abortion is permitted in special circumstances in India.

Genetic engineering

When President Clinton contacted many religious groups in America in March 1997 to find out their views about genetic engineering and cloning, Hindu opinions were divided. Questions were discussed, such as 'How much injury is permissible to clone a person or find a cure for cancer or blindness?' Some people say that any **himsa** is not acceptable, whilst others would say that the cancer itself is a form of himsa and needs to be removed.

Drugs

Ancient Hindus used a drug called soma as part of their worship, and some **sadhus** in India still use cannabis as part of their religious ritual. In Britain, however, the Hindu population respect the British laws and do not take drugs. Medicines are acceptable for health reasons. Smoking is allowed, but most devout Hindus do not smoke.

Many Hindus do not drink alcohol, but it is not expressly forbidden. Getting drunk in public would be disapproved of by the other members of the community. Alcohol and tobacco are usually banned in the mandir and in community rooms.

- Is it against Hinduism to have an abortion?
- Why do you think it is that most Hindus do not smoke?
- Do all Hindus believe the same things about sex, drugs and abortion?

For your dictionary

Himsa is an act of violence.
Sadhus are Hindu holy man.

Look back

1 Divide a clean page into two columns. In the left column, write the heading 'Hindu views' and in the right column write 'My views'. Write two sentences in each column about each of the following issues:

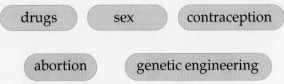

drugs   sex   contraception

abortion   genetic engineering

2 Imagine that you are the 'Agony Aunt' for a Hindu magazine for young people. Write a reply to each of the following letters:

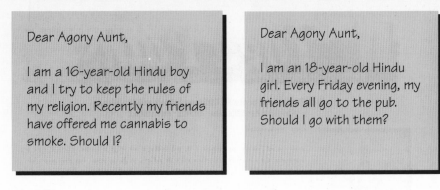

Dear Agony Aunt,

I am a 16-year-old Hindu boy and I try to keep the rules of my religion. Recently my friends have offered me cannabis to smoke. Should I?

Dear Agony Aunt,

I am an 18-year-old Hindu girl. Every Friday evening, my friends all go to the pub. Should I go with them?

3 If a person is religious, should their religion affect the way they behave?

Can you find Hinduism on the Internet?

The Internet is a good source of information on many topics, including Hinduism. It also allows Hindus from across the world to communicate with each other. There is enough information to keep anyone interested in Hindusim busy for weeks.

Home pages

The following sites may be of use, and many include links to other sites:

- Web sites for the Hare Krishna and ISCKON movements
  http://web.canlink.com/ocrt/hare.htm
  http://www.intnet.mu/harrish/text/krsna.htm

- A site which has updates on the latest additions to spiritual television and video
  http://www.webcom.com/itv/STOP.html

- Swaminarayan home page
  http://www.wp.com/AksharNet/SHM.htm

- The Hindu Universe
  http://www.hindunet.org/home.shtml

- Hindu Resources Online
  http://www.hindu.org

- Hinduism's Electronic Ashram
  http://www.HinduismToday.kauai.hi.us

- Spiritweb
  http://www.spiritweb.org

Or use a search engine and type in the word 'Hinduism' – you will get more 'hits' than you will know what to do with!

Why might a Hindu use the Internet?

http://www.spiritweb.org

Image Gallery: Vedic Deity

http://www.sudarsana.com

http://www.spiritweb.org

Yoga Paths. An Overview Of Different Schools and Traditions

http://www.HinduismToday.kauai.hi.us
© Hinduism Today, used with permission

These addresses were correct at the time of going to print, but they might change.

Chat lines

You might find the many 'chat rooms' useful for researching Hinduism. Most of the time the people you will 'chat' to are Americans; quite often they will be a devotee of ISKCON. These written 'conversations' are occasionally useful, but more often than not they have little to do with Hinduism as a belief. Sometimes they contain arguments, but even though they are not censored I have never found anyone on the line to be offensive.

Pinboards

If there is anything that you would like to know about Hinduism, you can leave a message on a pinboard and a week or so later you can look back to see if you have any replies from other users.

I have done this many times for Hinduism, with mixed results. A

question about modern-day Hinduism brought me no answers but a great many requests for more information! I have read pinboard messages about everything from Hindu belief in reincarnation to a conversation about the meaning of life.

Other uses

There are many other Internet applications: you can order Hindu resources, subscribe to the *Hinduism Today* magazine, or just read the many pages that are on the Web. You can even email the author of this book on dsymmons@exeter.ac.uk

⬐ Look back

Hare (page 65)
Krishna (page 13)
Reincarnation (page 5)

- What is a search engine?
- What would you do to leave a message for others to read?
- What would you do to get instant answers from Hindus?

Write an email message to a Hindu. What questions will you ask him or her? If you have Internet access, send the question to one of the Hindu email addresses or place it on a pinboard.

85

Holy books
What are shruti and smriti?

Hindus have many holy books. To help us understand how they are treated, we can sort them into two main categories: **shruti** and **smriti**.

- Shruti are 'those that have been heard'. The holy people heard the knowledge directly from Brahman and then passed it on from generation to generation. Only the brahmins learned the Vedas and they made sure that they were not altered in any way but learnt *exactly* as the first brahmin had heard them.

- Smriti are 'those that can be remembered'. Ordinary people would hear and remember stories, which they retold to their families. Some of these stories might change a little when one person told them to another, so smriti are not so highly respected as shruti.

Shruti

Shruti are very special holy books. Very few people can read them because they are written in sanskrit. When the priest reads them in the mandir, the words are sometimes translated afterwards as most Hindus do not understand sanskrit.

The books have been around for thousands of years and are extremely important in Hindu worship. In some mandirs the Vedas are kept in a glass cabinet to protect them.

Smriti

Smriti are also holy books, but they are treated in a different way to shruti. The stories have been translated into numerous different languages and are read by many people. They have been interpreted and studied by religious leaders and holy people, and they often come with a commentary to explain what is happening.

Some people like to learn passages 'by heart', plays and shows are sometimes performed in mandirs retelling the stories, and films and videos have been made. The **Mahabharata** was so popular when it was serialised in 92 episodes on television in India that it stopped the traffic in pollution-laden cities because everyone stopped to watch it.

If some of the story is changed a little, it does not offend anyone as long as the meaning is unchanged.

- What group do the Vedas belong to?
- Does it matter if the stories of the smriti are changed slightly?
- What group does the Ramayana belong to?

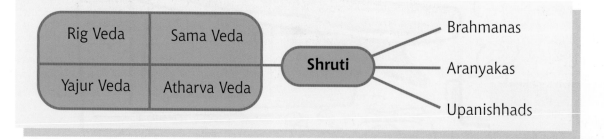

Rig Veda | Sama Veda
Yajur Veda | Atharva Veda — **Shruti** — Brahmanas / Aranyakas / Upanishhads

Ramayana — Puranas
Smriti
Mahabharata — Law

What do the words smriti and shruti mean?

Why do some Hindus keep their holy books in glass cases?

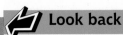 **Look back**

Aum (page 5)
Brahman (page 10)
Brahmin (page 7)
Mandir (page 9)
Ramayana (page 13)
Rig Veda (page 7)
Sanskrit (page 37)
Vedas (page 15)

For your dictionary

The **Mahabharata** is the great Hindu epic that relates the story of the battle between good and evil.
Shruti are the holy books believed to have been revealed by God to wise men.
Smriti refers to the scriptures that were 'remembered'.

The following words can be found across, down and diagonally in the wordsearch below.

a Copy the wordsearch carefully into your book. Then find each word, putting a circle around each one as you find it. The first one has been found for you.

b 23 letters are left. Write them down to make a sentence about the holy books.

Aum   Brahmanas   Law   Mahabharata   Puranas
Ramayana   Sama   Sanskrit   Shruti   Smrti
Story   Upanishads   Vedas

```
S A N A M H A R B
S H H S I N T D T
D Y R U A S A H I
A A R U V M R E R
H V M O T W A L K
S A E N T I H Y S
I H O D L S B Y N
N R A M A Y A N A
A B M U A S H O S
P P U R A N A S O
U K I T I R M S S
```

What are the Vedas?

The word 'veda' means 'knowledge'. The Vedas are a collection of four ancient holy books: the Rig Veda, the **Sama Veda**, the **Yajur Veda** and the **Atharva Veda**.

Rig Veda

This is at least 2,300 years old, making it the oldest of the books. It is divided into ten sections and contains more than 1,000 hymns. The hymns are written in sanskrit but recently some attempts have been made at translating the hymns into other languages. The most popular verse from the Rig Veda is the Gayatri Mantra (see page 40).

Yajur Veda

This Veda is a collection of special words which the priests use when they perform rituals. It is also the Veda which is most often recited when the havan is being used. The book is a collection from two sources: the older source is known as 'black' or 'dark' (because it is not clear what the meaning of the words is); the other source is known as 'white' because its meaning is understandable.

Sama Veda

This is the third Veda that contains words which could be set to music – the word 'saman' means 'to chant'. It is about half the size of the Rig Veda. The verses are sung to the gods Agni, Soma and Indra.

Atharva Veda

Some people say that the first three Vedas deal with the gods and this one deals with life. It tells us about magic charms, herbs for treating illnesses, spells for getting rid of evil spirits and how to conduct weddings and funerals.

Which holy book is used during ceremonies?

Each Veda contains four sections:

- The Samhita are the original writings of the Vedas and contain hymns, prayers and rituals.

- The Brahmanas is an interpretation and commentary on the Samhita.

- The Aranyakas were written by holy people living in the forests.

- The Upanishads are the secret and sacred messages of the Vedas.

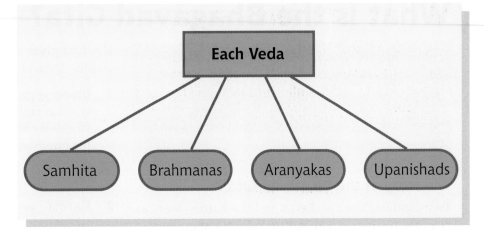

Copy this diagram into your book and write a sentence to explain each part of the Vedas.

- How many Vedas are there?
- Which Veda is the oldest?
- Why does one Veda have a 'dark' section?

Look back

Gayatri Mantra (page 41)
Havan (page 37)
Rig Veda (page 7)
Sanskrit (page 37)
Vedas (page 15)

1 a On a clean sheet of paper, draw a large version of this table:

Rig Veda	Yajur Veda	Sama Veda	Atharva Veda	All Vedas

b Write each of the following statements in the correct column in the table.

The name of this Veda means 'to chant'

Contains 1,028 hymns

Written in sanskrit

Contains magic charms

Has a 'black' collection

Has a 'white' source

Is half the size of the Rig Veda

Is the oldest of the Vedas

Contains Samhita and Brahmanas

Contains the Gayatri Mantra

Contains the secret and sacred Upanishads

It is about 2,300 years old

Used in rituals with the havan

Contains hymns to Agni and Indra

Tells you how to use herbs to cure illnesses

2 The Vedas are believed to contain all the information you need to live your life. Think of ten rules or pieces of good advice that you would put into a book to guide other people in their lives.

What is the Bhagavad Gita?

The Bhagavad Gita is a very important Hindu holy scripture. It is one small part of a much larger book called the Mahabharata. The Mahabharata is possibly the world's longest poem, and it is believed to contain more than three million words.

The story of the Bhagavad Gita

Two families, the Pandavas and the Kurus, were at war. On the battlefield at Kurukshetra, members of each family were getting ready to fight. Arjuna, the leader of the Pandavas, was filled with sorrow at the thought of seeing his family killed to gain a kingdom:

'How shall I fight... with arrows on the battlefield?... I will not fight!' (Bhagavad Gita 2:4,9)

He turned to his chariot driver, Krishna, for guidance. Krishna talks to Arjuna and it is this conversation which makes up the Bhagavad Gita.

Krishna gives Arjuna three main reasons why Arjuna should fight:

1   Jnana-yoga – striving for the knowledge of what is right and what is wrong. Krishna stressed that Arjuna's atman and the atmans of his enemies would never die but would be reincarnated. Therefore, to kill is only to kill the body, not the soul.

2   Karma-yoga – it is Arjuna's duty to be a warrior and to fight.

3   Bhakti-yoga – it shows his devotion to Krishna to fight.

Arjuna agrees to go into battle and goes on to defeat the Kurus.

Meaning

Most Hindus do not think that the battle in the Bhagavad Gita is an earthly battle. The battle that Arjuna and all Hindus must fight is against the temptations of this world.

Krishna tells Arjuna why he should be prepared to fight. What were the main reasons he gave?

This picture shows Krishna as Arjuna's chariot driver. Why do you think Krishna appeared to Arjuna at this time?

- Where did the battle in the Bhagavad Gita take place?
- Why did Arjuna say 'I will not fight!'?
- What were the three reasons he was given to show that he had to fight?

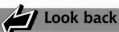 **Look back**

1 Read this quotation by a Hindu to explain the meaning of the story:

'The story of the Bhagavad Gita is still relevant today. For example, if you were tempted to take drugs we could use Krishna's three arguments:

- *You must fight for the knowledge of what is right and what is wrong.*
- *You must follow your path of duty and fight the temptation to copy your friends.*
- *You must be devoted to God and fight the temptation to forget Him. If you remember God, you will not want to take drugs.'*

Give four other examples of the things that a Hindu today might have to fight.

2 Arjuna had a debate with Krishna. How do religious people today know what is the right thing to do?

3 Why do some people think that resisting temptation is similar to fighting?

4 Some Hindus liken the battlefield in this story to everyday life. Arjuna did not want to fight his relatives and friends; he was in danger of giving up his faith rather than fight them. Can you think of a time when you have had to make a choice between fighting temptation or giving in and doing what other people wanted? Did you give in?

What is the Ramayana?

The Ramayana is a popular Hindu holy book. You have already read part of the story on pages 18 and 19. On these pages you can read the rest of the story.

The story continues

A great bird saw that Ravana had kidnapped Sita. The bird attacked Ravana but was struck down by a vicious blow. The bird fell to the ground and was discovered by Rama and Lakshmana. In its dying breath it told them that Sita had been kidnapped. Rama and Lakshmana made their way through the forest towards Sri Lanka – the home of the evil Ravana.

As they wandered through the forest, **Hanuman** and his army joined Rama and Lakshmana in their search for Sita. They had many adventures, including killing a one-eyed ogre. Eventually they arrived at the coast and, seeing Sri Lanka in the distance, asked the sea god for safe passage across the water. In some versions of the story, this is refused and they build a bridge of arrows across the sea.

Across the waters a great battle took place. Ravana, the ten-headed evil king, and his soldiers fought Rama, Lakshmana, Hanuman and their soldiers. The battle went on for a long time. Many people were killed but in the end Ravana was destroyed.

Sita was rescued but Rama was not certain that she had remained faithful to him. To prove that she was still pure and loyal to Rama, she put herself into a fire. When she stepped out unhurt, everyone was sure that she had remained loyal.

Reunited, they all walked back to Kosla, their home country. As they approached the borders they were a little anxious. Some years before, Rama had been banished to the forest, and

Who was Ravana?

Who was Hanuman?

 Look back

Diva lamp (page 27)
Rama (page 13)
Ramayana (page 13)
Sita (page 19)

For your dictionary

Hanuman was the monkey warrior who faithfully served Rama and Sita.

Bharata, his youngest brother, was to rule in his absence. Would they be welcomed back, or would they have to fight to regain the kingdom?

As it grew towards dusk, they walked over the hill which led into their kingdom and a wonderful sight met their eyes. In every house in the land a diva lamp had been lit to welcome them home.

Rama, Sita, Lakshmana and Hanuman walked to the palace. They soon found out that while they had been away Bharata had put a pair of Rama's shoes on the throne, to show that Rama was really the king.

- Where did Ravana take Sita when he kidnapped her?
- Why did Sita step into the fire?
- How did the people make Rama know he was welcomed home?

1 If you started a puppet production of this story on pages 18 and 19, act out the rest of the story.

2 Here is a list of the main events in the story. Write them down in the right order and then draw a picture to go with each one.

The sea god lets them cross to Sri Lanka
Rama kills Marich, the deer
They fight an ogre in the forest
They are welcomed home by thousands of diva lamps
Hanuman joins Rama and Lakshmana
Rama, Sita and Lakshmana go to live in the forest
Sarup Nakha meets Rama
Sita proves her purity in the fire
Ravana is angry when he listens to his sister
The bird tells Rama that Sita has been kidnapped
Ravana takes Sita to his castle on Sri Lanka
Ravana is killed in a long battle
Sita is tricked out of the magic circle

3 After hearing this story, Hindus might think about what it means to them today. Below are six statements. Each could be used to teach us something about how we should live our lives. Copy each statement and then explain what it teaches people today.

a Bharata did not take control of the country but waited for Rama to come back.
b The bird died trying to save Sita.
c Hanuman and his army remained loyal to Rama
d Sita was tricked by Ravana.
e Ravana acted out of revenge.
f Sita remained pure.

What other holy books do Hindus have?

Hindus have many other holy books. Some are connected to the Vedas and others are written by or about their gurus. Some Hindu teachers have written books to help guide other Hindus.

A story from Srimad Bhagavatam

A dwarf went to King Bali and asked that he grant him as much land as he could cover in three paces. Bali was amused by the request and offered the dwarf a whole island but the dwarf insisted on just as much land as he could cover in three paces. Bali promised the dwarf the land. The dwarf grew to a huge size and in one step covered the earth, in the second step he covered the heaven and in the third step he covered the rest of the universe. Bali humbly kept his promise.

The Laws of Manu

There is no person called Manu; the word simply means 'man'. Sometimes this collection of 12 books is known as 'Manu-smriti' or the 'Code of Manu'. It is a collection of religious rules for Hindus and it is at least 1,700 years old.

The Puranas

This is a collection of books which are about 1,000 years old, although some of them were written only 400 years ago. They help the priests to lead worship to the various gods. The books are often in the form of a conversation between the god and a holy man.

In the Agni Puranas we are told about the god's wife and his three sons. He is described as dressed in black, with smoke as a banner, and carrying a fiery javelin. He has four hands and rides a chariot whose wheels are the seven winds.

Changes

Within Hinduism, smriti books may well appear to be constantly changing. The stories are told over and over again and most Hindus do not seem to mind if they are retold in different ways. The names of the characters change and sometimes the god in the story will be changed to another god. This might seem confusing but, as all the gods are really Brahman, it is not important.

The smriti books are there to help Hindus understand and experience Brahman. If the details are changed to make them more relevant to one particular group of people, it does not really matter. Recently many of the stories have been retold in story books. The pictures may not completely match the pictures that the original authors had in mind, but the books help us to understand the stories. The stories are often performed in dance. Each of the movements of the dancer tells part of the story. Sometimes it is the eyebrows, sometimes the smile, sometimes the positions of the fingers that retell the events in the story.

Why did the king laugh at the dwarf?

Why is dance a good way to tell stories from the scriptures?

 **Look back**

Brahman (page 10)
Guru (page 53)
Smriti (page 87)
Vedas (page 15)

- What are the Laws of Manu?
- What are the Puranas?
- Why do some of the stories keep changing?

1 The story of the dwarf is a story with a meaning.
a Read it again then sit quietly for a short while to try and understand what the meaning might be.
b Draw a picture of the dwarf stepping over the earth and write a description underneath about what the story means to you.

2 a Think about performing a dance version of the story of the dwarf. Consider each of the moves necessary to retell the story clearly. For example, the first scene could be a nervous dwarf arriving at the castle asking to see the king – how would you show nervousness?
b Find or compose some music to accompany your dance, then rehearse, perform, and video it.

Index

Page references in bold indicate that the word is defined on this page in the 'For your dictionary' box.